SHORT • SCENIC • WALKS
AMBLESIDE &
SOUTH LAKELAND
PAUL HANNON

HILLSIDE PUBLICATIONS

2 New School Lane, Cullingworth, Bradford BD13 5DA

First Published 2020   © Paul Hannon 2020

ISBN 978 1 907626 27 2

Sketch maps based on OS 1947 1-inch maps

Cover illustrations: Yewdale; Great Langdale
Back cover: Wastwater; Page 1: Grasmere from Loughrigg Terrace
(Paul Hannon/Yorkshire Photo Library)

Printed in China on behalf of Latitude Press

HILLSIDE GUIDES... cover much of Northern England

• 50 Yorkshire Walks For All   • Journey of the Wharfe (photobook)

Short Scenic Walks • Wharfedale & Ilkley • Harrogate & Nidderdale
• North York Moors • Ambleside & South Lakeland • Teesdale & Weardale
• Bowland & Ribble Valley • Aire Valley • Haworth • Hebden Bridge
• Upper Wensleydale • Lower Wensleydale • Swaledale • Malhamdale
• Sedbergh & Dentdale • Ingleton & Western Dales • Around Pendle

Walking in Yorkshire   • Wharfedale & Malham
• North York Moors South & West   • North York Moors North & East
• Nidderdale & Ripon   • Three Peaks & Howgill Fells
• Harrogate & Ilkley   • Wensleydale & Swaledale
• Aire Valley & Bronte Country   • Howardian Hills & Vale of York
• Yorkshire Wolds   • Calderdale & South Pennines
• South Yorkshire   • West Yorkshire Countryside

Lancashire/North Pennines
• Bowland • Pendle & the Ribble • Eden Valley • Alston & Allendale

Visit us at www.hillsidepublications.co.uk

Colwith Force

Wasdale Head

CONTENTS

Introduction.........................4

1 River Kent.......................6
2 Orrest Head..................8
3 School Knott..................10
4 Windermere Shore........12
5 Latterbarrow..................14
6 Scandale.....................16
7 Lily Tarn.......................18
8 Rydal Water..................20
9 Loughrigg Terrace......... 22
10 Alcock Tarn...................24
11 Helm Crag.................... 26
12 Silver How................... 28
13 Loughrigg Fell...............30
14 Little Langdale............. 32
15 Great Langdale.............34
16 Tilberthwaite Gill............36
17 Holme Fell.................. 38
18 Tarn Hows....................40
19 Monk Coniston............ 42
20 Coppermines Valley.......44
21 Coniston Water............. 46
22 Beacon Tarn.................. 48
23 Stickle Pike................... 50
24 Wallowbarrow Gorge....52
25 Hardknott Castle...........54
26 River Esk...................... 56
27 Blea Tarn (Eskdale)........ 58
28 Wastwater.....................60
29 Lingmell Gill.................62
30 Blea Tarn (Langdale)......64

INTRODUCTION

With its combination of mountain peaks and beautiful lakes, the Lake District is England's most impressive national park, and this guide offers 30 moderately undemanding outings within its southern half. The bustling little town of Ambleside is the focal point for South Lakeland, much as Keswick is for North Lakeland. Ambleside sits at the head of England's largest lake, Windermere, and within a stone's throw are the poet Wordsworth's Grasmere, and charming Elterwater at the entrance to rugged Langdale. A little further are Coniston and Hawkshead, past which are the more remote valleys of Eskdale, Wasdale and the Duddon.

Within these pages you will walk the shores of Windermere, Coniston Water, Wastwater, Grasmere and Rydal Water, and visit iconic landmarks such as Tarn Hows, Helm Crag and Wasdale Head - along with lesser known gems such as Colwith Force, Scandale and the Wallowbarrow Gorge. The easily attained viewpoints of Orrest Head, Latterbarrow and School Knott offer sweeping panoramas over Windermere, while enchanting lower fells such as Silver How, Loughrigg Fell and Holme Fell offer rather more challenging little climbs; jewelled tarns set amid colourful slopes include Alcock Tarn, Beacon Tarn, Lily Tarn and two Bleas Tarns. And if these wondrous natural features are not enough, you will also discover a Roman fort, abandoned coppermines and slate quarries, packhorse bridges and a narrow-gauge railway.

Whilst the route description should be sufficient to guide you around, a map is recommended for greater information and interest: Ordnance Survey Explorer maps OL6 and OL7 cover all the walks.

●Lake District National Park Authority
Murley Moss, Oxenholme Rd, Kendal LA9 7RL (01539-724555)
Information
●Central Buildings **Ambleside** LA22 9BS (0844-2250544)
●Victoria Street **Windermere** LA23 1AD (015394-46499)
●Glebe Road **Bowness-on-Windermere** LA23 3HJ (0845-9010845)
●Ruskin Avenue **Coniston** LA21 8EH (015394-41533)
●Old Town Hall, The Square **Broughton-in-Furness** LA20 6JF
(01229-716115)
●Main Street **Hawkshead** LA22 0NS (015394-36946)
●26-28 Finkle Street **Kendal** LA9 4AB (01539-735891)

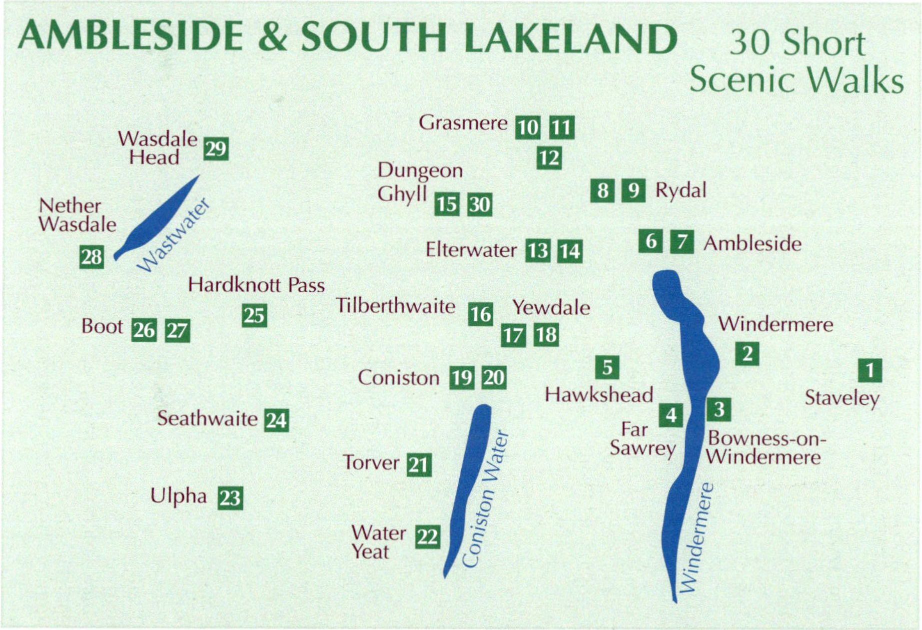
AMBLESIDE & SOUTH LAKELAND
30 Short Scenic Walks
Wasdale Head 29
Nether Wasdale
28
Wastwater
Grasmere 10 11
12
Dungeon Ghyll 15 30
8 9 Rydal
Elterwater 13 14
6 7 Ambleside
Hardknott Pass
25
Boot 26 27
Tilberthwaite 16
Yewdale
17 18
Windermere
2
1
5
Coniston 19 20
Hawkshead
Staveley
4
3
Far Sawrey
Bowness-on-Windermere
Seathwaite 24
Torver 21
Ulpha 23
Water Yeat 22
Coniston Water
Windermere

4³4 miles from Staveley

Woodland and riverbank in unsung surroundings

Start *Village centre*
(SD 471981; LA8 9LR),
roadside parking
Map *OS Explorer 7,*
English Lakes South East

Staveley village features the Eagle & Child pub, Hawkshead Brewery's Beer Hall in the Mill Yard, a Post office/shop, a rail station and the 15th century tower of St Mary's church. Leave the street by an enclosed path between the Mill Yard and the tower, running to a footbridge crossing the River Kent. A few yards downstream, take a wallside path left to an access road at farm buildings. From a bridle-gate opposite, a path rises through trees and on to join a back road. Go right to a fork, then rise left. Quickly reaching a sharp bend, take a bridle-gate into Craggy Plantation. A good path rises away right, and after an early zigzag slants gently through beeches to the wood edge. It then rises steeply with the enclosing wall, soon gaining the top corner with views to the Kentmere fells.

Swinging left the path begin an extended, undulating stroll close by the wood top. Initially above a few crags and dropping slightly, remain on this to reach a square cairn. From here the path descends a few stone steps to swing right to a gateway in a wall. The beechwood is traded for mixed woodland as you continue, dropping a little to a stile at the far end: super views return ahead. Turn right through a gateway and follow a faint path up the field to a skyline stile. Resuming, a slight rise leads on to a stile on the very brow. Look back to a mountain panorama with the Coniston and Langdale fells prominent. Resume downhill, trading wallsides at another such stile, and a grassy track drops down to the rear of Littlewood Farm. Pass through the gate and yard onto a back road.

Turn right for a largely unfenced ten minutes. Immediately after a gate across the road take a grassy wallside bridleway rising left to cross an access road to a gate outside a wood edge. The enclosed path rises very slightly before commencing a sustained descent outside Mike's Wood. At the bottom a gate puts you into the wood of Spring Hag, and a broader path resumes. Lower down it becomes surfaced and leaves the wood to drop down onto a back road. Go briefly left to a second access point on the right into the Woodland Trust's Beckmickle Ing. A path runs downstream with the Kent for a few minutes to Hagg Bridge. Across this farm bridge turn right to commence a return upstream. Close by the river for some time, a fine early barn precedes a knoll, then across to a gate sending a direct march across a field to a ladder-stile.

Briefly rejoining the river on a bend, go straight on through a gateway and a field centre to a stile into trees back by the river. Emerging at a stile, the path again cuts a corner, briefly meeting again through a gateway at a bend just around which is a gate. Head away along a wallside past a moist spring, with an enclosed cart track forming at the end. This runs to a bend where you forsake the track for a kissing-gate to the left. Through it turn right with the wall and across to a corner kissing-gate onto an enclosed pathway. Go right to a road, and right on the footway back into the village. The later stages see you off the road in the company of the river.

River Kent

3$\frac{1}{2}$ miles from Windermere

A meandering stroll to an iconic Lakeland viewpoint

Start Rail station (SD 413986; LA23 1QA), car park nearby
Map OS Explorer 7, English Lakes South East

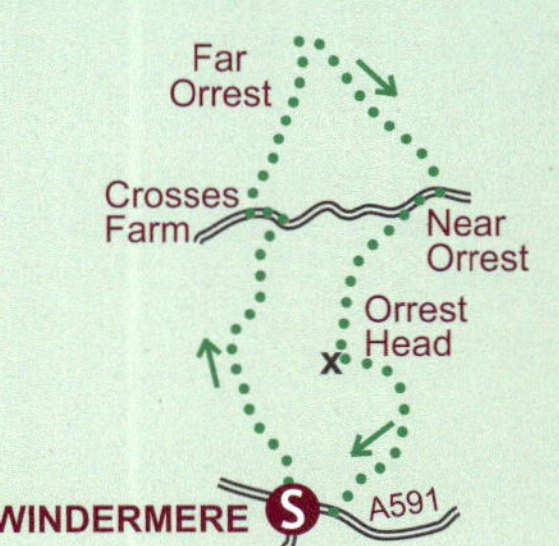

Windermere grew with the arrival of its branch line in 1847, and remains many visitors' arrival point into Lakeland. Cross the adjacent A591 to the Windermere Hotel, to the left of which an Orrest Head sign points along an access road. Rising away, fork left on an enclosed path. Opening out on a wooded bank, ignore a right branch on a brow just before houses. Your path remains enclosed for some time, crossing three driveways before entering a small wood. Drop down behind a house, and just beyond a right fork, a path bears off right through a small gate into High Hag Wood.

The path runs to a kissing-gate into a field. Rising gently away, as it forks keep right near the wall to a kissing-gate outside the wood. Through this go left with the wall to one into Low Hag Wood. Joining another path, bear right along the wood edge onto a back road. Go left to Crosses Farm, then take the short drive to the last house. A gate to its right sends a grassy track away with a wall to your left. Rising gently across the field centre, it reveals a view to the Coniston and Langdale fells beyond Windermere.

Through a gate at the end remain with the wall, and approaching the next gate/stile Far Orrest Farm appears. Part way on the next fieldside the track bears right towards it, through a gate in a dip to rise to the farm. Through a gate into its confines, turn right up to another into the farmyard, then left a couple of strides out onto an access track. A couple of yards right take a gate above, and bear right over a small enclosure to a gate onto a walled way.

From another small gate in front, turn right along the field edge to a gate onto a track at the end of the farm. From a gate opposite, a path heads away with a wall on your right. From a gate at the end bear left across a field to locate a wall-stile, and resume with the wall on your left. At a bend cross a stile and a field towards Near Orrest. From a stile right of a gateway, a short path runs through trees towards the rear of the buildings. Bear right outside them on a short track, but quickly leave by a bridle-gate to the right. A path then runs left along the field edge to a stile onto a back road.

Go right a short way to a stile by a gate on the left. A grassy track heads away, crossing a streamlet by ford or slab bridge, and resuming with a wall to your right. The way starts rising pleasantly, briefly levelling before climbing to a top corner stile. A path rises through open country, either branch at a fork leading up to the crest of Orrest Head. At 781ft/238m this splendid viewpoint is famed as guidebook writer Wainwright's first Lakeland experience. A mountain panorama from Coniston Old Man to Ill Bell is ranged beyond Windermere. From the high point go left on a grassy path into trees, and down to a bottom corner wall-stile. From a kissing-gate on the right a path briefly drops then levels out to run through Common Wood to a gate back out. Head away with a wall to your right, down to become enclosed at the bottom. Dropping to a gate onto the A591, cross to the footway and go right to finish.

Orrest Head

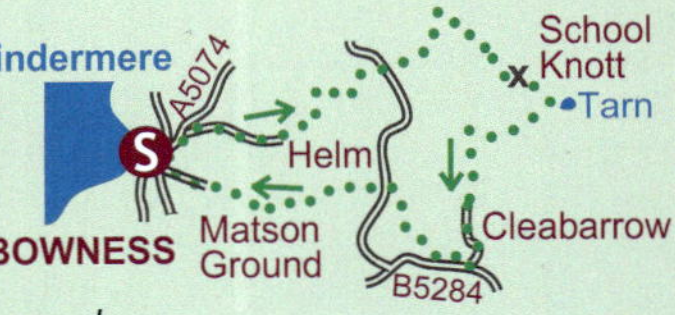

4³4 miles from Bowness-on-Windermere

A classic viewpoint

Start *The Promenade (SD 401968; LA23 3HJ), car park*

Map *OS Explorer 7, English Lakes South East*

Bowness stands midway along the lake's eastern shore: various craft ply the waters, including a car ferry to the Claife shore. With your back to the boat landings go left on Lake Road, rising to a junction at the Albert and up past shops to escape right up Helm Road. Climbing steeply out of town, higher up a parallel path runs along a wood edge on the left. Rejoining the road at the top, fork right and over a crossroads to rise to Helm Lodge. Keep left, running on to rise by a wood with big views beyond housing, soon reaching Helm Farm. As the onward track bends sharp right, take a path left by trees, then on alongside a field. At the end turn right on another path in front of houses, curving round above them to a wooded bank. Within a minute take a lesser path right: immediately forking, the right one leads up through trees into a small pasture. The path rises past Lickbarrow to a kissing-gate onto a back road.

From a gate opposite follow a wall away, later dropping left and on to a stile/footbridge at the end. Rising onto an access road go left past Old Droomer, with suburbia again on your left. At a gate into scattered woodland, bear right on a grassy path rising to a kissing-gate onto the base of School Knott. Go briefly right then take the grassy path rising left. This splendid short ascent forks right over a streamlet and winds up to a small cairn by a rash of stones: bear right and close by a solitary tree to gain the summit's modest rock slabs. At 761ft/232m this unsung Lakeland viewpoint boasts a stunning mountain panorama beyond Windermere.

Depart by continuing your ascent line, a grassy path aiming for School Knott Tarn in its hollow beneath Scots Pine. Through a gate the path drops towards the foot of the little tarn, a lovely spot. The path resumes with the tiny outflow down to a corner gate into gorse. It drops gently down across a stream and onto a broad, level track. Double back left for a level stroll, alternatingly enclosed and open. A final gate joins an access road at Cleabarrow, leading out to the B5284. Turn right on a parallel path, rejoining the road to escape right on a driveway. Approaching Low Cleabarrow drop left to a gate, then descend a fieldside to kissing-gates in and out of trees. From another one ahead rise diagonally up the slope, between trees on a brow to drop to another kissing-gate. Cross the next pasture to a brief narrowing, then bear left to a kissing-gate behind a stand of larch. Cross straight over a back road and down an enclosed path to an access road junction at Matson Ground.

Cross to a kissing-gate and on to another, then on beneath trees past a pond. Another such gate puts you onto another drive: go briefly right, then take a path left through trees to a gate into a field. A path crosses to a gate in the far corner, then left onto an enclosed way to a drive. Cross and along an equally short way to a gate into a field top. A firm path descends its right side to kissing-gates either side of a cart track. Continue down the final pasture to a stone 'Dales Way' seat: Windermere's upper section now points to a mountain skyline. At the bottom a gate admits to the head of Brantfell Road, whose footway leads down into the centre. At the bottom cross over and down St Martin's Hill onto the outward road opposite the church, and go left to finish.

School Knott Tarn

3^{1}2 miles from Far Sawrey

Lakeshore and woodland on the quieter side of Windermere

Start Ash Landing (SD 387953; LA22 0LW), National Trust car park on B5285 just west of ferry
Map OS Explorer 7, English Lakes South East

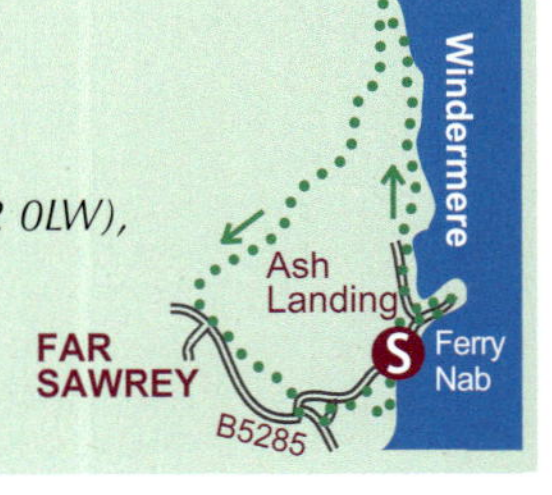

A broad path leaves the north end of the car park into trees. Quickly forking, take the left branch climbing slate steps to a fork at an information panel. Though your onward route is right, first spiral briefly left to the folly directly above. Claife Viewing Station dates from the 1790s, built as a summer house with extensive views over Windermere. Steps to the upper floor still provide that glorious panorama over massive reaches of England's largest lake. Back on the path, this winds down beneath the viewpoint to run through a courtyard with café onto a back road. The ferry terminal, former Ferry Hotel and WC are along to the right at Ferry Nab, reached partly by a footpath. Going left the road runs along the shore to Harrowslack car park. From here open grassy swards save you treading tarmac on a pleasant course above the shore. Alongside is the largest of Windermere's islands, richly-wooded Belle Isle.

After a mile by the lake, leave as the road enters woodland at a cattle-grid: a half-minute further, a bridle-path doubles back left through the trees. After a spell by the wood edge it commences a sustained but pleasant climb. Higher up, ignore a level branch left and continue a little further to a boulder seat beneath a clearing at the top. The path rises by a wall before tapering walls usher it out of the trees at a gate. It runs a pleasant course to the walk's high point as a branch path goes left down to the ferry. Your path runs into the open to quickly reach a track crossroads. Go straight on through the gate ahead, soon commencing a steady wallside descent with Near Sawrey visible ahead beneath the Coniston Fells. Joining another track from the right above the old vicarage, it swings left through a gate to run on and down to the B5285 in the sleepy hamlet of Far Sawrey. Directly below you is the Cuckoo Brow Inn, while St Peter's church is further along a side road.

Without joining the road take an access road rising left. At the top a kissing-gate sends a path along the front of a large house (Sawrey Knotts), then on a driveway towards a lone house. With stables on your right, keep straight on to a bridle-gate ahead. The wallside path drops down to another drive at another house, then straight on down a broad path back onto the B5285. Cross and rise a few yards right to turn off across the Cunsey side road, with more of the lake in view. At an early junction double back left to rejoin the B5285: a bridle-gate on the right sends a parallel enclosed path down a fieldside to a gate back onto the road. Whilst you could cross and conclude on another parallel path down through the trees, preferably take the large gate on your side into Ash Landing Nature Reserve. Immediately forking, take the right one along the wood top, soon curving left at the end and downhill, then back along the bottom near the shore. Passing a tiny pond at an information panel, leave by another tall gate back onto the road. The lakeshore is alongside, and the car park immediately in front.

Windermere from the Viewing Station

4½ miles from Hawkshead

Beautiful woodland and pastures either side of a pocket fellwalk

*Start Village centre (SD 352981; LA22 0NT), National Park car park
Map OS Explorer 7, English Lakes South East*

Hawkshead is a pretty village, its shops, pubs and cafes watched over by St Michael's church. From the south end of the main street turn left on the Sawrey road, and over Pool Bridge bear left on the slender Wray road. Keep left at a junction into the scattered hamlet of Colthouse. As the road bends sharp right, go left on stony Scar House Lane to commence a hedgerowed stroll. Soon reaching a cross-path, a small gate on the right sends you up a steep pasture to cross to a kissing-gate into Crag Wood. A super path heads away through springtime bluebells, rising slightly then running on by the left edge. A little short of the wood end, fork right on a thinner but clear path: it rises slightly to run a super course close by the left edge, at the end emerging via a kissing-gate onto Loanthwaite Lane.

Turn right to a T-junction, then left just as far as a gate on the right. A good path rises away to begin the ascent of Latterbarrow. Soon forking amid scrub, the left branch ascends colourful slopes with magnificent views over colourful country to the Coniston and Langdale fells. A stone built section features before the going eases, and the massive summit monument is revealed. The path runs a gentle five-minute course to gain the 800ft/244m summit, only at this moment revealing Windermere ahead. Leave by a broad path heading north-east to a superior viewpoint for Windermere backed by the Fairfield Horseshoe. The descent path winds down to a gate into scattered trees, dropping to a fence/wall corner at the wood edge. The path remains in the trees to drop to a fence-stile with a forest road behind. Go left the short way down to a gate onto a firmer access road, and left, out of the wood down onto a road at High Wray. Go left, with Blelham Tarn seen to the right.

After a memorial fountain of 1891 drop right down a lesser road to pass Hole House in a dip. Remain on the road rising back left, but go right at a short drive to High Tock How. Don't enter but take a gate on the left and ascend the short fieldside: ignoring a gate at the top, turn briefly right to a gate at a wall-kink. Through it advance a few strides then turn sharp left across the field, soon bearing right as the wall bears left. This grassy way crosses past a minor marsh in a hollow, and on to neighbouring stiles in a corner.

Drop right with a hedge over a drain, then bear left to a gate across the field. Head away with a hedge on your right, and maintain this course as a cart track forms at a gate to lead to Loanthwaite Lane. Go left past High Loanthwaite farm, and just beyond, take the first of adjacent paths signed right. A broad path heads away with a hedge, shortly passing through a gate in it. A thinner path resumes on its other side, down through kissing-gates back onto Scar House Lane. Go briefly left, then a bridle-gate on the right sends a firm path across to another before a path junction. Bear right to a T-junction by Black Beck, then left as far as a bridge over it. A broadening lane leads onto the B5285: cross to re-enter the village.

3¹4 miles from Ambleside

An easy walk into a lovely wooded valley

Start *Town centre
(NY 376045; LA22 9BS), car parks*
Map *OS Explorer 7,
English Lakes South East*

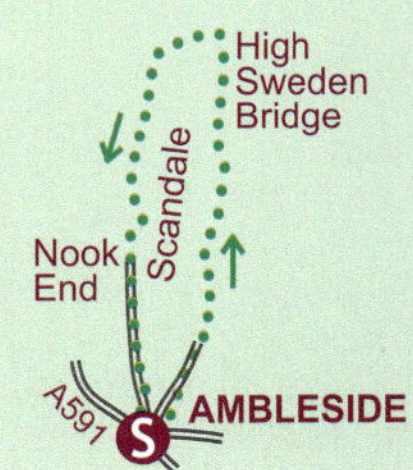

Ambleside is one of the Lake District's major centres, a busy little town abounding in eating places, gift shops, pubs, and most of all, outdoor equipment shops. Features of interest include the tiny, two-storey Bridge House astride Stock Ghyll: even the stairs are outside. It houses a National Trust information room, while across the main road is a waterwheel on the beck. Other notable features are St Mary's church with its tall spire, and a cinema. A mile south at Waterhead are the remains of the Roman fort of Galava, various boat trips on Windermere, and a youth hostel.

From the Market Cross head along North Road past the information centre, and immediately over the bridge on Stock Ghyll turn right up Peggy Hill, a footway between cottages. Bear left at the top onto Chapel Hill, then rise right into a square with a former church. Go sharp left out onto another road, Smithy Brow, and straight across along Sweden Bridge Lane. Ignore an early fork left, and remain on this as it climbs away past exclusive residences. It's uphill all the way, ignoring a right fork towards the top by a Victorian postbox. The tarmac finally ends when a gate signals its continuation as an enclosed cart track.

The track continues to rise, bringing fine views ahead to various peaks of the Fairfield Horseshoe. Further to the left are High Raise, Langdale Pikes, Bowfell, the Coniston Fells and the head of Windermere: Rydal Water is also seen backed by Silver How. The way rises more gently before it swings pleasantly into enchanting woodland at the narrow neck of Scandale. The track runs unfailingly on above tumbling Scandale Beck, making a short pull past old quarries reclaimed by nature. After levelling out again look down on a waterfall below, then a final pull reveals High Sweden Bridge just in front. Fork left to this elegant stone-arched structure whose idyllic setting demands a break before crossing it. If wishing to extend the walk, continue upstream as far as you like on the continuing track into the sanctuary of Scandale.

From adjacent bridle-gates across the bridge, go a few yards downstream, then fork right on the stone-built path ascending by a wall to a ladder-stile in a wall at the top. Rise a few feet further onto a level track. Turn left on its part grassy course, through a gateway by stone sheep pens. Advancing, ahead is a great prospect over Ambleside to the extensive waters of Windermere backed by wooded Claife Heights. The track underfoot remains your splendid route all the way now. Across to the right, the Langdale Pikes put in an impressive appearance. The track gradually winds down to cross Scandale Beck on stone-arched Low Sweden Bridge. Across it is Nook End Farm, from where follow Nook Lane back. This runs on above some university buildings, and slants down to emerge onto Smithy Brow just below the Golden Rule pub. The main road into the centre of Ambleside is just yards below.

Bridge House,
Ambleside

**3¹⁄4 miles
from Ambleside**

**Low-level fellwalking on
the broad flanks of Loughrigg**

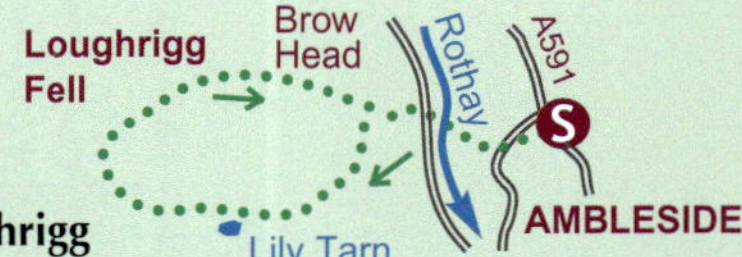

Start *Town centre (NY 376045; LA22 9BS), car parks*
Map *OS Explorer 7, English Lakes South East*

For a note on Ambleside see page 16. From the Market Cross head down Compston Road opposite, and part way down turn right on Vicarage Road. This swings left to run between church and school to become a surfaced path into Rothay Park. Advance on this same path to the end, where stone-arched Miller Bridge leads onto a narrow road. Turn right over a cattle-grid then quickly left up a drive, steeply up to a cluster of houses at Brow Head. Losing its surface on a hairpin bend immediately above, take a wall-stile on the left. A path runs briefly through woodland to a small footbridge onto the lower flanks of Loughrigg Fell. An immediate right fork ascends bracken slopes, steadily rising left after the wall bears away right, and up to a kissing-gate in a wall above. With the climbing done, this is a good place to enjoy the superb panorama of fells including Helm Crag, the Fairfield Horseshoe, Ill Bell and Wansfell, as well as Ambleside itself.

The path continues past a reedy pool (ignoring a left branch) and quickly on to the more sizeable Lily Tarn. Ahead are the Coniston and Langdale fells, featuring the Old Man, Crinkle Crags, Bowfell and Harrison Stickle. Though not accorded such status on the map, the commonly regarded top of Todd Crag is the knobbly crest hidden back to the left: a path heads towards it, to be rewarded with an unrivalled view of Windermere's extensive upper reach, part of a memorable panorama.

Back at the tarn, resume along the main path on its right bank, continuing along a broad ridge. Soon closing in on a wall to the left, all-round views include a section of Windermere back to the left. The largely level, grassy path runs on past a tiny reedy pool, and with a shallow depression on the right, gaps in the wall offer optional access to the knolls atop the 'official' Todd Crag. This looks down over steep and rough partly wooded slopes to Clappersgate and the tree-rich environs of the Brathay. The river leads the eye to Great Langdale, where the high peaks of Crinkle Crags and Bowfell complement the Langdale Pikes.

The main path, meanwhile, never strays far from the wall. Dropping slightly to a kissing-gate in a fence, rejoin the wall after skirting a small marsh at a fork: ahead are Loughrigg Fell's seemingly vast flanks. The path is ushered right by the wall to slant down to cross well-defined Troughton Beck. Just up the other side the broad Skelwith Bridge-Ambleside bridleway is joined. Turn right on this to re-cross the beck on stepping-stones beneath a reedy pool, then rising slightly to a brow beyond. Simply remain on this broad way to a gate off the open fell, then dropping gently by a wall in rough pasture that was once a golf course. Becoming firmer this drops through a gateway and past a modern house at Pine Rigg. Now surfaced, it drops down to a gate where it becomes enclosed to descend back to Brow Head. Conclude as you began back to Miller Bridge and Rothay Park.

Lily Tarn

3¹2 miles from Rydal

A simple circuit of a beautiful small lake

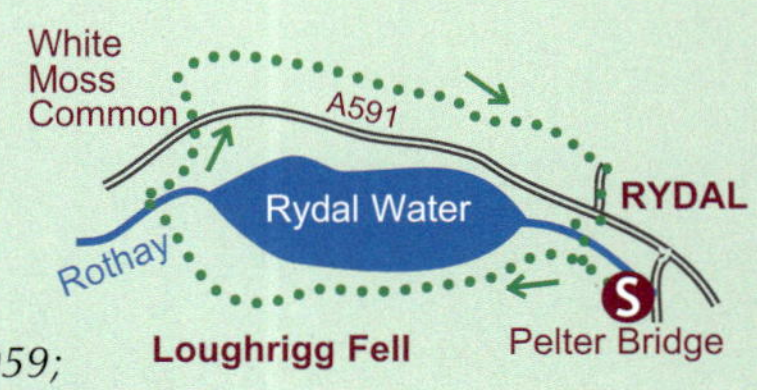

Start *Pelter Bridge off A591 at Rydal (NY 364059; LA22 9LW), National Park car park*
Map *OS Explorer 7, English Lakes South East*

From the car park resume along the short-lived road rising past houses to continue as a walled track. This runs on to drop to a gate onto the base of Loughrigg Fell, with Rydal Water outspread just ahead. This beautiful little lake is surrounded by woodland and fells: in its centre is wooded Heron Island. With an immediate fork, take the right branch dropping to the shore. A lovely section leads along, and after a while is deflected left by walled pastures, rising slightly then running on to the start of White Moss Wood. Take the gate into the trees and the path heads away, soon dropping left to arrive at a shapely footbridge on the River Rothay.

Across, turn right on the path downstream past a popular grassy riverbank area. At a major fork go left to a WC, immediately past which, with a car park just ahead, take a left branch the few strides up onto the A591 on White Moss Common. Cross with care to a postbox and go very briefly left, then bear right up a broad way into trees. This rises to join a surfaced access road in front of a house. Your return route is along the Coffin Road, at one time the last journey of Rydal's dead bound for Grasmere churchyard.

Turn right, soon losing its surface but continuing for some time beneath steep slopes and around inflowing Dunney Beck. The lane abruptly ends at an unexpected and very isolated house. The thinner but still broad continuation ignores a branch path dropping right, and commences a foolproof, near-level course along the slopes. Simply remain on this path all the way for a glorious stride beneath the steep, rough flanks of Nab Scar. The path runs through scattered trees and colourful terrain, and later emerges into open pastures to finally earn stunning views over the lake beneath Loughrigg Fell. At the end the path rises slightly to a gate, from where its walled course leads out above Rydal Mount onto an access road. Rydal Mount was the home of William Wordsworth from 1813 to 1850, and with its attractive gardens and tearoom is open to the public.

Turn right down the steep road to emerge back onto the A591 alongside Rydal Church. St Mary's dates from 1842 and features a Millennium Garden, while on its other side is the National Trust's Dora's Field, a celebrated location of daffodils. From the churchyard a little network of paths work their way around this part wooded bank and down onto the main road. Either way, turn right on the road the few strides to the Glen Rothay Hotel, with its Badger Bar. Directly opposite, a path drops to cross a sturdy wooden footbridge on the Rothay, then immediately forks. Take the left branch rising to a bridle-gate into trees, and rising left the short way up to another onto the lane on which you began. Turn left for two minutes back to the start.

Rydal Water

4¹4 miles from Rydal

A celebrated promenade and a famous lakeshore

Start White Moss Common (NY 350065; LA22 9SD), car park with WC below A591, a mile west of Rydal
Map OS Explorer 7, English Lakes South East

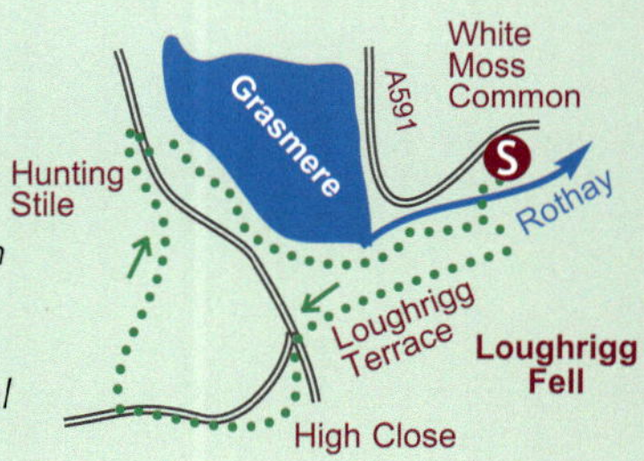

From the end of the car park take the lower path through trees, meeting the River Rothay to reach a shapely footbridge. Across, take the path rising gently through White Moss Wood, keeping left to a gate onto a broad path on the foot of Loughrigg Fell. Turn right for a short wallside pull onto a brow with glimpses of both Rydal Water and Grasmere. At this major path junction, take that rising gently left. This is the start of Loughrigg Terrace, a classic way that enjoys an undemanding slant across the flanks of the fell, savouring unfolding Vale of Grasmere views. At the end you enter trees at a kissing-gate: keep left at this fork, rising gently between walls. Just a minute further is a second fork, where rise left through a gateway and then along to a gate onto the Red Bank road.

This junction is marked by guidestones set in either wall. Here take a small gate straight ahead into High Close Arboretum. A firm path heads away, but quickly leave on one dropping left to rapidly meet a broader path: go right through the youth hostel's extensive grounds. Ignore lesser branches as it undulates through shrubbery, then on above a pond with the hostel up to the right. Reaching a wall enclosing Low Wood, simply remain on the broad path swinging up to the right to a gate onto a driveway alongside the house, and go left the short way out onto the Red Bank road. Turn left over the cattle-grid into open country, soon swinging round over a bridge with excellent views over the Elterwater scene.

As the wall drops away, remain on the road a short way to a point where a path crosses it. Turn right, the path climbing steeply to quickly ease out on the crest of this ridge dividing the Brathay and Rothay valleys. Cross the broad brow, ignoring a left branch climbing away. A sturdy wall comes down from the left to run to a bridle-gate at the end, with Grasmere village and vale appearing ahead. With walls set back either side, the path negotiates a marsh before a nice descent with the wall to your right. In the bottom corner you become enclosed at a gate, with a seat and lake view. Ignoring branch paths either side, commence a long, steady descent between walls to the house at Hunting Stile. Its driveway continues down the short way further onto the Red Bank road.

Go briefly right until a gate on the left sends an enclosed bridleway down to the lakeshore. Here it turns right to commence a super lakeside walk, later passing through Deerbolts Wood and out to an open area back on the base of Loughrigg Fell at the lake-foot. Continue past the outflow weir and an immediate footbridge, remaining on the path alongside the Rothay. Through a bridle-gate this enters White Moss Wood to run a broader course downstream, back to the footbridge just five minutes from the start.

Grasmere from Loughrigg Terrace

3³4 miles from Grasmere

Outstanding paths make light work of a climb to a hidden gem

Start Village centre (NY 336076; LA22 9TA), car parks
Map OS Explorer 7, English Lakes South East

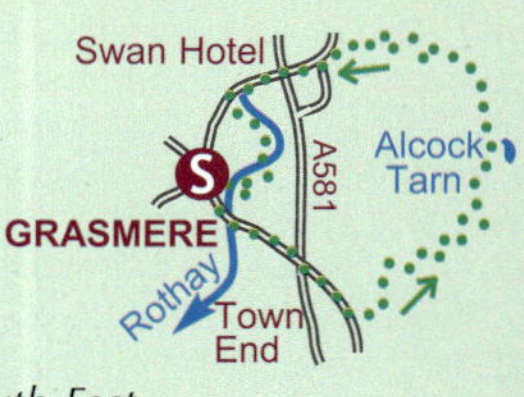

Grasmere is equally famed for its natural beauty and its literary connections. William Wordsworth, most famous of the Lake Poets, was buried in St Oswald's churchyard in 1850 beneath the plainest of headstones. Alongside is the long-established Grasmere Gingerbread shop, a tiny 17th century building that was once a school where he and his sister Dorothy taught. Grasmere's annual Sports feature Cumbrian traditions such as fell running, hound trailing and Cumberland & Westmorland wrestling.

From the southern end of the green make your way the short way to the church, and head out along Stock Lane (the Ambleside road) to the A591 roundabout at Town End. Cross to the back road opposite, passing Dove Cottage. Best known of Wordsworth's Lakeland homes (1799 to 1808), it is a popular visitor draw. Rise past the cottage to a reedy mire on open ground, and turn left up the near side. As the driveway ends, bear right on a path scaling the wooded bank to a seat by a rising road. Turn left here on a track rising to a gate into the wooded grounds of Brackenfell. The continuing track soon rises to a gate out into more open country.

Rising through scattered trees, another path joins at a bend as you spiral uphill to pass a stone walled pond. Fading tree cover permits unfolding views of the Grasmere scene as the path slants up the fellside. A small gate in a sturdy wall is reached just past a second well-placed bench, with Crinkle Crags and Bowfell joining the Coniston Fells and Langdale Pikes from possibly the best of all Vale of Grasmere viewpoints. The path rises above a final stand of larch and up to cross a streamlet on a tiny stone-arched bridge.

Another spiral leads onto the rocky knoll of Grey Crag, with Windermere's extensive waters joined in the view by Coniston Water. Behind the knoll the path runs through a gateway to reveal Alcock Tarn reposing serenely on its shelf. This attractive sheet of water was formed by a grassy dam at this near end.

Resume along its bank to a small gate, passing a reedy pool to begin the descent. With deeply set Greenhead Gill in front, the path is another gem, its well-made zigzags cheating the gradients. The path drops past a wall corner and down to another enclosing a plantation. It descends outside the trees and above the beck to double back down to a footbridge across it. Just upstream the Thirlmere aqueduct crosses the beck, taking Lakeland rainwater to Manchester. Turn downstream to a gate off the fell alongside a house, and a narrow, surfaced drive shadows the beck down onto a back road. Go left to swing round to meet the A591 at the Swan Hotel. Cross straight over and down Swan Lane into the village.

A nice finish takes a gate into the park on the left after bridging the Rothay. A surfaced path heads away to join the river, turning downstream to Broadgate car park. Cross the footbridge and resume downstream, ignoring a private bridge then crossing the next to trace the other bank. This curves round, ignoring another footbridge and ushered away from the river to emerge back into the centre alongside the Wordsworth Daffodil Garden.

Alcock Tarn

4¹⁄4 miles from Grasmere

A short, steep pull on a good path to a favourite Grasmere landmark

Start Village centre (NY 336076; LA22 9TA), car parks
Map OS Explorer 7, English Lakes South East

For a note on Grasmere see page 24. From the green cross to the left of the Heaton Cooper studio, where a cul-de-sac lane leaves a crossroads. Becoming a drive approaching Allan Bank, over a cattle-grid turn right on a firm path, with Helm Crag rising ahead. From a kissing-gate an enclosed path parallels Easedale Road, joining it at Goody Bridge. Across the bridge keep straight on at the junction, shortly emerging into a field to cross to the group of dwellings of Far Easedale. Bear right on the continuing rough track, rising to a gate just past the last house. Turning left, within yards a fork of walled ways is reached and the climbing begins.

The right branch rises the short way between walls onto the base of Helm Crag. Turning right it quickly spirals back up alongside an old quarry, and a steep wallside pull leads to more open surrounds. Swinging left beneath craggy outcrops, it winds splendidly up high above Far Easedale. With Grasmere's lake an early feature, the waterfalls of Sour Milk Gill are a permanent attraction across Easedale. A grassy section slants right to arrive benath the ridge-end, with a beautiful view into the Vale of Grasmere. The final pull is a short, lively clamber through outcrops (or a simpler path to the left) before the summit ridge is gained.

Helm Crag's intriguing felltop demands careful exploration. The summit is a double ridge with a low trough in between. The highest point of 1328ft/405m is at the far end, where a tilted rock tower known as the Howitzer points skyward: an adventurous scramble is required to claim the true crown. Helm Crag is known to travellers on the A591 as the Lion and the Lamb: it is the grouping of rocks first encountered that earn this title. Before leaving, note that returning the way you came avoids a steep descent.

Beyond the base of the Howitzer advance a few steps to a cairn above a rocky bluff. Drop left onto the onward path down to another cairn, before a short descent into the saddle of Bracken Hause. As the path starts to re-ascend, locate a grassy branch left through bracken. This runs to overlook a steeper drop, then sets about its descent. Slanting right then more firmly left, it drops to cross a streamlet near a wall corner. Continue down to a grassy knoll, but drop right by the wall, leaving its corner and curving left to arrive above another wall just below. Bear right above it and conclude the descent by crossing a small marsh as the resuming grassy path drops the short way onto a bridleway in Far Easedale.

Turn left alongside Far Easedale Gill, becoming more enclosed along the base of Helm Crag to rejoin the outward route. Go through the gate to the head of the road, and this time take a path through a gate on the right (not the farm road doubling back to Brimmer Head). An enclosed path winds round to a gate into a field, across which it crosses stone-arched New Bridge. Joining another broad path turn left, crossing the field into trees hiding a footbridge on Easedale Beck. Rejoining the outward route, turn right to retrace opening steps.

Helm Crag from Grasmere

3¹4 miles from Grasmere

**A delightful climb on good paths
serving a famous Grasmere felltop**

*Start Village centre (NY 336076;
LA22 9TA), car parks*
*Map OS Explorer 7,
English Lakes South East*

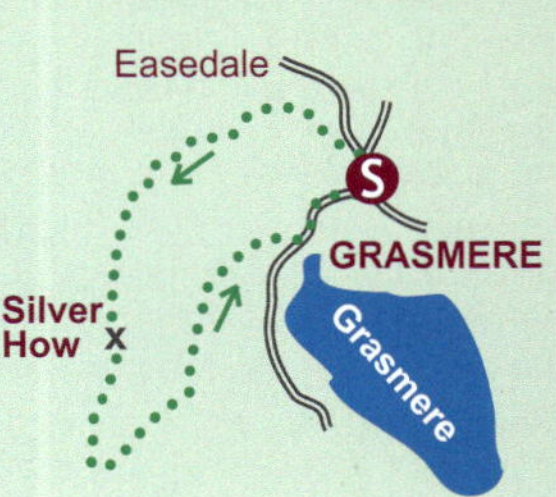

For a note on Grasmere see page 24. From the green cross to the left of the Heaton Cooper studio, where a cul-de-sac lane leaves a crossroads. Within a couple of minutes it transforms into a parkland drive, with your objective rising to the left. Approaching Allan Bank (one of Wordsworth's former homes), stay on the drive bearing right and continue uphill to its demise at an enviably sited house. Already there are fine views over the Vale of Grasmere, from Helm Crag round to Fairfield. Without entering, take the short driveway left to a gate. A fieldside path rises away, becoming enclosed and winding up to emerge onto the open fell. The path continues its climb, close by the wall on your left. Grasmere's lake appears down to the left, though it will soon be better seen. Higher, just before the wall swings away left, follow the main path slanting right, soon ascending more gently through scattered juniper with a small gill to your right. Before long it swings left to a large cairn just beneath a knoll overlooking Grasmere's lake and village.

The path continues on the near side of the knoll, over a cross-paths to meet Wray Gill on your left. Turn upstream for less than 100 yards, then take the left branch down to cross the briefly tamed ravine in colourful surrounds. Exiting via rocky slabs, the path rises into an upland basin revealing the final slopes further ahead. A large cairn is passed on a sustained gentle rise to the foot of the uppermost slopes, then a short, steep pull past a sprawling cairn quickly finds you gain the summit cairn. At 1296ft/395m this fine felltop reveals a stunning array of hills, from the Coniston and

Langdale fells around to the Helvellyn and Fairfield groups. Equally impressive is the glorious prospect of lakes, featuring Grasmere and Rydal Water in virtual entirety, also Windermere, Loughrigg Tarn, Elterwater and a tiny glimpse of Coniston Water.

Leave by continuing south across the gently declining summit crest, a path quickly materialising to enter bracken on the Grasmere side of the hill. This makes a pleasant, gentle descent towards a substantial cairn on a grassy plinth. The path drops to its right down a small hollow to bring Chapel Stile in Great Langdale into view immediately below. Within two minutes you meet another path, where go left for a further minute's traverse down to a cairn at a cross-paths on extensive level ground. This marks the high point of a path linking the Rothay and Brathay valleys.

Turn left here to commence the return. This calls for little description, the path being clear throughout with ample opportunity to appraise Grasmere's lake in its green vale. The well graded descent passes the remains of a rifle range target, and keeps just above a dense zone of juniper before meeting a wall beneath Silver How's steep flanks. This ultimately ushers the path down to a corner kissing-gate, then it winds down two varied enclosures before dropping to a bridle-gate. The now enclosed path descends onto the Red Bank road opposite Grasmere's boat landings. All that remains is a short walk left back into the village.

The Langdale Pikes from Silver How

4 miles from Elterwater

A delectable little fell amid magical countryside

Start *Village centre (NY 327047; LA22 9HP), National Trust car park*
Map *OS Explorer 7, English Lakes South East*

Elterwater is a lovely slate village with the Britannia Inn and a café set back from a small green. From the green turn into the car park, where a gate sends an enclosed path downstream with Great Langdale Beck. Leaving the beck it runs into woodland with glimpses of Elterwater, shortly after which take a left fork up to a gate onto the B5343. Cross to a path into trees, rising right to emerge via a bridle-gate onto a colourful common. Go left, rising gently and quickly absorbing another path to trace the boundary wall to a brow, revealing Loughrigg Tarn backed by Loughrigg Fell. The path winds right down towards the rear of a white house, where fork left down onto its access track. Go left on this to a cottage at Loughrigg Fold, swinging right onto a minor road.

Go briefly left and leave by a stile on the right. Cross to a stile in the wall ahead, close by the tarn shore. Ignoring the lower path, rise steeply left as a path forms to run to a gate onto an enclosed track in front of a house. Go briefly left, and shortly after a second house, a path slants right up to a gate onto the base of Loughrigg Fell. The path slants gently up alongside a wall as far as a gate. Here branch right to commence your ascent of Loughrigg Fell, a good path making relatively light work of a sustained climb. Near the top the going eases and a grassy conclusion leads to a prominent cairn. Just a minute further is a path junction in a hollow surrounded by minor knolls: take the broad path left the short way to the OS column at 1099ft/335m. Only now does the Vale of Grasmere appear, along with Windermere and Esthwaite Water.

Depart by the main path heading north towards Grasmere, but leave within a couple of minutes: after a short, stony drop, a sizeable boulder and sprawling cairn on your right sit just yards beyond a faint grassy way bearing left. This drops onto a minor knoll, below which it becomes clearer to commence a delightful descent. It winds surprisingly quickly down, with Grasmere's lake returning in style. Passing right of a wall corner the path descends between wider spaced walls to a kissing-gate in a fence, beneath which it drops onto a back road.

Go left to a gate on the right into High Close Arboretum. A broad path heads away through extensive grounds, swinging left at a near immediate fork. Ignore lesser branches as it runs through shrubbery, then on above a pond with a youth hostel up to the right. Reaching a wall enclosing Low Wood, simply remain on the broad path swinging right up to a gate onto a driveway alongside the house, and go left the short way out onto the Red Bank road. Turn left over the cattle-grid into open country, soon swinging round over a bridge with excellent views revealing the Elterwater scene. Just below, a path drops left with the wall, then runs steadily across to rejoin the road. Without setting foot, take a grassy path dropping left onto the B5343. Cross straight over on a short section of path onto the road into the village, with the centre just ahead.

Langdale from Loughrigg Fell

4³4 miles from Elterwater

Lake and waterfalls in rural idyll

*Start Village centre
(NY 327047; LA22 9HP),
National Trust
car park
Map OS Explorer 7,
English Lakes South East*

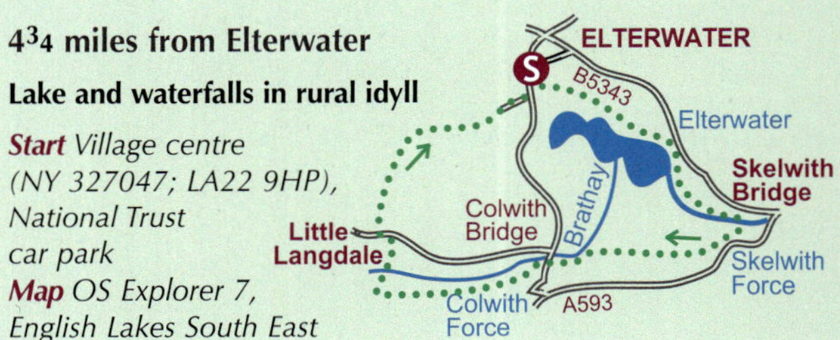

From the green with the Britannia Inn and a café set back, turn into the car park where a gate sends a path downstream with Great Langdale Beck. Leaving the beck it runs into woodland before emerging at the foot of Elterwater, a beautiful moment with a neatly framed view of the Langdale Pikes. A path resumes with the outflowing River Brathay through open pasture. Re-entering woodland cross the footbridge on the river, noting that 100 yards downstream is Skelwith Force, its lack of height compensated for by its ferocity as water surges through a narrow rock passage. A little further is a café, with the Skelwith Bridge Hotel just beyond.

The path rises away left and curves through trees to a junction: keep right, up to a kissing-gate out of the wood. A firm path crosses a field onto an access road, where turn right the short way down to Park House. Through kissing-gates to the left the path resumes across open pasture, then on through a gate to rise to Elterwater Park (Park Farm). At the other side, ignore the drive left and take a continuing path straight ahead. This runs to a stile in a wall, and on to another just below, where it becomes briefly enclosed. Emerging by the cottage of Low Park, from a stile ahead the path curves across a field to a stile above a steep wooded bank of the Brathay. The path descends steps to head upstream, out of the trees and along to a stile onto a road at Colwith Bridge. Go briefly right, but before the bridge take a stile into trees up to the left. Take the right-hand path quickly slanting left over tilted slabs and pleasantly along with the Brathay to soon reach a splendid viewpoint for the magnificent spectacle of Colwith Force.

Leave by a stepped path fifty yards before the falls, running on precariously above another viewpoint and a 'money tree'. A spell by the beck precedes a slant left up through beeches. At the top it runs on through trees to a gate into a field. Follow the wall away, passing through a gate in it and crossing to enviably sited High Park. A gate puts you into its yard, where refreshments may be available. Pass between the buildings to gates onto a road on your left, and go right for a few minutes to Stang End. From a gate on the right behind the buildings, an enclosed path descends to a gate into a field, then down to a footbridge on the Brathay. Ascend the field behind to a kissing-gate onto the road in Little Langdale.

Go left 50 yards to Wilson Place Farm, with the Three Shires Inn just 100 yards further. Turn up the near side of the farm, and through a bridle-gate on the right at the edge of the yard. A path ascends the fieldside and on to a kissing-gate at the end, followed by a brief enclosed spell. Emerging, the path goes briefly left then across the reedy pasture to a kissing-gate onto a rough road. Turn right and simply remain on this, soon entering woodland as it works its way stonily down. Ultimately become surfaced, a little further down it joins a road opposite the Eltermere Inn. Go left to be finished within five minutes.

Elterwater

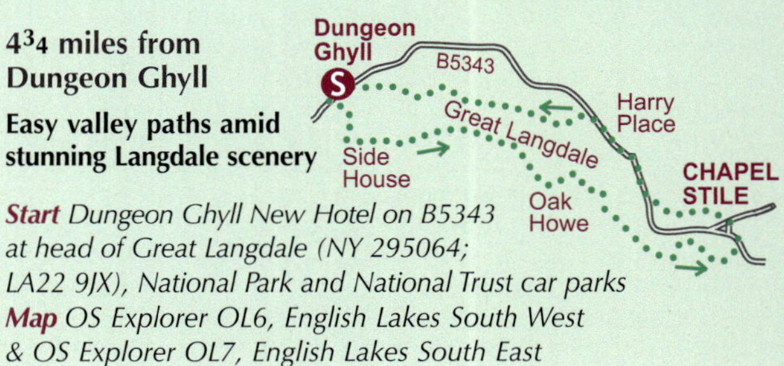

4¾4 miles from Dungeon Ghyll

Easy valley paths amid stunning Langdale scenery

Start *Dungeon Ghyll New Hotel on B5343 at head of Great Langdale (NY 295064; LA22 9JX), National Park and National Trust car parks*
Map *OS Explorer OL6, English Lakes South West & OS Explorer OL7, English Lakes South East*

Dungeon Ghyll is at the heart of the Langdale scene, with the Stickle Barn pub alongside the New Hotel. From the drive go on the front of the Stickle Barn into the NT car park. Head out onto the road, and go left just a few strides to a gate on the right, from where an access road crosses fields and Great Langdale Beck into the yard at Side House. Bear left to a kissing-gate onto the foot of open fell, and joining a path across a footbridge go left with the streamlet. Passing through a gateway and along to a gate, a stone-pitched path ascends to an old sheepfold at the top corner. Across a streamlet a path resumes along the slope, steadily dropping to run above a wall. Glorious Langdale views include carpets of springtime bluebells. Beyond a gate in an intervening wall you enter a part-walled way meandering along to a fine barn. At this path junction, go left past the barn to the house at Oak Howe.

Follow the drive out to Great Langdale Beck, and ignoring a footbridge, remain on the track swinging right. A grass embankment makes a nicer surface as you are joined by Baysbrown drive. With Chapel Stile just ahead, the drive crosses New Bridge on the beck and swings right beneath slate spoilheaps. As it turns left for the road keep straight on a walled path to Thrang Farm. Go straight ahead on the access road, and at a junction at a small green, again go straight ahead, narrowing to emerge onto a tiny common. Just a little further you join the B5343 opposite WCs in Chapel Stile.

Chapel Stile is a little village of which much originated to accommodate workers in its nearby slate quarries. Holy Trinity church looks over from a natural platform, while to your right is Wainwrights Inn. Turn left into the centre, and just past the shop and cafe, turn right the short way to the church. Go left in front of it, passing a memorial well of 1887. Ignoring the road dropping left, rise past the final cottages to a gate into a former quarry site. A path runs on above a wall into the heart of this fascinating area, and it clings to the boundary wall to emerge by a covered shaft on a low knoll at the end. Suddenly back into untainted surrounds, the Langdale Pikes loom powerfully directly ahead. A contrastingly grassy track drops down behind cottages to emerge via a gate back onto the B5343.

Turn right for a few minutes, past the old farm of Harry Place and gently dropping down. Ignoring a first bridleway left, a minute further turn left down a walled track. Quickly reaching a junction on crossing a streamlet, this old road swings right for a long, steady stride along the flat dale floor. The charismatic Langdale Pikes are supported in this dalehead parade by Crinkle Crags and Bowfell. Towards the end it joins the beck, then bridges Stickle Ghyll before emerging into the car park across the road from the New Hotel.

Chapel Stile

3 miles from Tilberthwaite

An impressive ravine amid copper workings on Wetherlam's flanks

Start *Low Tilberthwaite (NY 306010; LA21 8DG), National Park Tilberthwaite Ghyll car park off A593 at High Yewdale*
Map *OS Explorer 6, English Lakes South West*

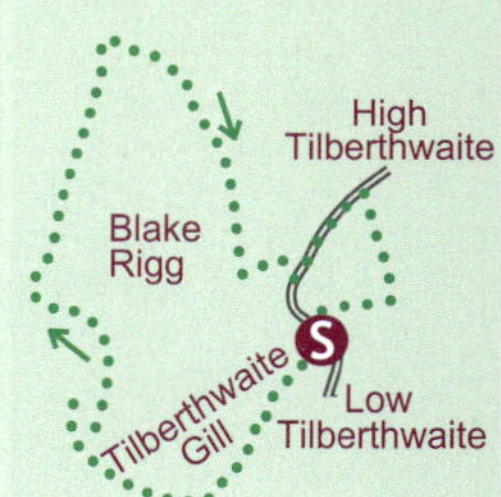

From the parking area return briefly along the road then double back right up an initially grassy old quarry track: this at once absorbs the more demanding slate steps from the car park. The old way slants up past old quarries on your left with the ravine of Tilberthwaite Gill below. The quarry scene is left behind on reaching a fork by a hut. Ignore the inviting green level branch running in to the gill and continue climbing. The path soon traverses a few rocky yards in a corner before easing and running more openly above the gill, with Wetherlam's bulky slopes above.

Continuing, the path swings round to a fork, where bear right to natural stepping-stones on Crook Beck, southerly feeder of the gill. The path now runs right across moister ground to a foot-bridge on Henfoot Beck, the northerly feeder. Alongside is a stone-arched level. Over the bridge advance a short way on the path running to meet a mine track, and double back left up it. It swings left above sizeable Tilberthwaite Copper Mines to rise to an upland plateau, then curves right for a short, stony rise to a large cairn. Continuing left of a rocky, larch-crowned knoll, it rises gently above Dry Cove Moss towards a cairn just short of another mining site.

Immediately before the cairn rise right to a fenced shaft abutting a crag, and rise right of it on a faint path onto larch-draped Hawk Rigg, the walk's high point. The little path drops to a fence corner, where drop briefly right and along the edge of a minor trough beneath larches to stiles at a fence junction. Ahead is a glorious prospect to the Langdale Pikes. With the fence now on your right, advance briefly to where it turns sharp right, then take the path slanting gently right down towards a sturdy wall. Double back right on this over a minor brow to approach a junction with that fence.

Just to your right a contouring green path runs to a stile in the fence to head away through a shallow trough, soon crossing the streamlet to join the wall. A better path continues, reaching a knoll revealing the Tilberthwaite area below. Remain with the wall as the path becomes firmer and the going steeper, descending by the ravine of Blake Rigg Gill to a stile in the wall near the bottom. Through it a faint grassy way descends the pasture, swinging left at the bottom around to a track. This drops right to Low Tilberthwaite: through the gate pass the houses with a spinning gallery to join the access road. While the car park is just to the right, preferably go left on the road to High Tilberthwaite, and just before the farm take a gate on the right. A grass track heads away with the wall to a gate, then across a field centre to a gate into Low Coppice. Ignore the track heading away and turn immediately right up a briefly rising path, continuing along the wood edge to drop to a kissing-gate out of the trees. Go right with Yewdale Beck to the start.

Tilberthwaite

3¹2 miles from Yewdale

**Superb walking on and
around a colourful little fell**

*Start Glen Mary Bridge on A593
north of Coniston (SD 321998;
LA21 8DP), National Trust car park
Map OS Explorer 7,
English Lakes South East*

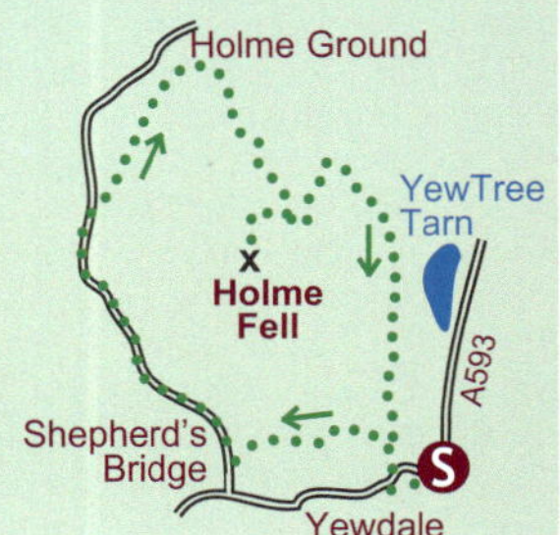

From a tiny parking area just west of the main one, cross a footbridge to a bridle-gate sending a concession path on the field bottom opposite Yew Tree Farm across the road. Soon reaching a kissing-gate, double back a few yards on the road and turn down to the farm with its spinning gallery. Without entering, a bridle-gate on the right sends a broad, firm path away, curving left above the farm to split at the start of open ground. That to the right is your return, so for now advance straight on past the farm with the rugged Yewdale Fells backed by lofty Wetherlam ahead. This splendid way undulates beneath Holme Fell's craggy buttresses to emerge onto the Hodge Close road at stone-arched Shepherd's Bridge.

Turn right for a long half-mile, often in the company of lively Yewdale Beck. After a rise away from it, a gate on the right sends a good track rising steadily with a wall through trees. Narrowing to a path, it emerges to cross open pasture with Holme Ground farm below. At the hairpin bend of a green track climbing from it, keep right on the upper branch rising to a gate in a wall. Through this your ascent begins by taking the thinner but still very clear path branching right. This rises through bracken to quickly reach a brow overlooking a broad hollow, with Holme Fell straight ahead.

The path skirts the right and far sides of the marshy hollow, then makes an easy ascent up colourful slopes. Towards the top note the cairn on Ivy Crag to your left, sometimes mistaken for the summit. As the undulating upper reaches are gained, take a thinner, grassy right fork to cross to a modest trench under the craggy summit ridge. Just to your right scale a small slab and the path doubles back left to rise onto the elongated, broad summit ridge, and just a little further the cairn stands at 1040ft/317m on a tilted slab. The rich panorama extends from the bulk of adjacent Wetherlam to the full length of Coniston Water, while northwards is a superb array of mountains from the head of Langdale to the Helvellyn, Fairfield and Ill Bell ridges.

Return to the little trench and advance the short way towards Ivy Crag. With a reedy pool to your left, take the path between it and Ivy Crag, dropping pleasantly left to soon fork. The right branch drops the short way to the grassy saddle of Uskdale Gap, a delectable spot marked by a cairn and traces of an old wall. From this path junction turn right, an initially grassy path entering scattered Harry Guards Wood for a steady drop, generally angling right. Lower down, a large clearing affords a good prospect over Yew Tree Tarn. Passing a large boulder, the path runs level to the right before the final drop to the valley. Joining another path, turn right past massive twin boulders to quickly reach a kissing-gate out of the scattered trees. The pleasant, level path crosses bracken pasture to a kissing-gate in another fence. A wall leads it on the short way to rejoin the outward route above Yew Tree Farm.

Yew Tree Tarn

4 miles from Yewdale

Delightful paths lead to and from a favourite attraction

Start Glen Mary Bridge on A593 north of Coniston (SD 321998; LA21 8DP), National Trust car park
Map OS Explorer 7, English Lakes South East

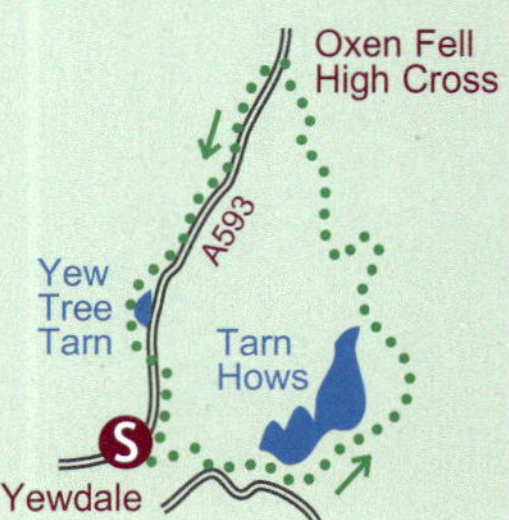

From the rear of the car park a broad path heads away, rapidly turning left on a broader way. This rises steadily, and after a brief pull leave by a gate on the left. A grassy track rises away, along a colourful pasture, zigzagging to the right near a ruin, then slanting left again. Good views look back to Coniston Old Man and Wetherlam. Slant left up by a crumbling wall leading to a gate into scattered trees, then rising steadily with a wall again to a gate at the top. A minute further, Tarn Hows is revealed just in front.

This is a splendid moment as you appraise one of Lakeland's most popular 'chocolate box' scenes. Originally an area of marsh and pools known as The Tarns, it was dammed over a century ago by the Marshalls of Monk Coniston Hall to power a sawmill, and the whole area was ambitiously landscaped. Beatrix Potter's acquisition of the estate in 1929 saw it passed on to the National Trust. The grassy slopes overlooking the tarn enable it to be viewed as a foreground to a fine mountain backdrop.

Joining a hard path drop left towards the shore. Don't pass through the gate but take the path right, undulating across grassy slopes above the tarn and soon rising above trees onto a broader path. Go left on this for a sustained walk above the eastern shore. Rising to a cross-paths in trees keep straight on, curving around the wooded edge and dropping to a footbridge at the tarn's northern limit. Here leave the circuit path by a fence-stile on the right, and a good path heads away across bracken slopes. Rising gently, it swings right to curve around to a gate onto the old walled lane of Oxen Fell Road. Turn left on this cart track, which remains underfoot for a considerable and splendid time, soon dropping steeply left and opening out with fine views left to Yewdale Fells. Ultimately merging into a narrow access road, continue down this the short way to the A593 by a cottage at Oxen Fell High Cross.

Cross to a minor road opposite and turn immediately left through a kissing-gate. A good path runs a parallel course with the road, on through a gate and entering woodland to run on towards Yew Tree Tarn. In the trees in front of it a circuit path is met. Ignore the footbridge left and bear right, the briefly grassy path at once forking. Ignoring that running to a gate in a wall ahead, go left, the path soon firming up again to run through colourful woodland just above the shore. At the end turn left over the dam to approach the road. The tarn was, like the walk's principal feature, created by damming a marsh. Without joining the road take a path dropping right after the outflow, running a briefly tight wallside course to emerge onto the road. Cross to a path opposite and turn right, ignoring a near immediate fork left. This path runs just above the road the short way back to the start, crossing a footbridge to finish.

Tarn Hows

4¹2 miles from Coniston

Easy walking blending lovely woodland with open views on the Monk Coniston estate

Start Village centre (SD 301975; LA21 8DU), National Park car park
Map OS Explorer 7, English Lakes South East

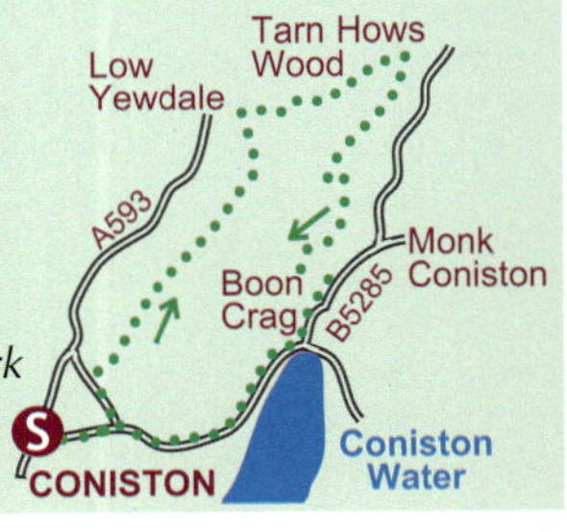

Coniston is a bustling village in an idyllic setting, with shops, pubs and cafes, as well as St Andrew's church and the Ruskin Museum. Its slate buildings shelter beneath towering fells crowned by Coniston Old Man, from whose slopes much of the slate was won. Leave the centre by the B5285 past the church, passing the Crown Hotel to a junction at Yewdale Bridge. Turn left, past a sports centre and on a little until level with a school. Here turn right over a bridge on Yewdale Beck, then immediately left over a stile for a few yards upstream. A kissing-gate leads into a sloping field, where the path rises left. A short line of trees leads to a corner, continuing to a kissing-gate at the end alongside the Dog Kennel. Built for foxhounds by the Marshalls who acquired Monk Coniston estate in 1835, a century later it was bought by Beatrix Potter and passed to the National Trust: it now serves as a shelter.

The path rises behind the folly to a wall-gate, continuing up to a fork. Ignoring the right branch, advance up between dense gorse. From a kissing-gate in a wall ahead the path runs through short-lived Back Guards Plantation. Ignoring a forest track right, emerge via a gate into the open. A pleasant path heads away with super views left to the craggy Yewdale Fells. Declining steadily through a long pasture the path fades: keep towards the right side, until at the end bear left over a rough track to a gate in a wall ahead. Cross the field centre to a gate at the far end onto a walled track: go left, dropping to trace Yewdale Beck upstream to a bridge at Low Yewdale.

Don't cross, but from a kissing-gate in front head around the fieldside. At the end the beck is briefly rejoined in Tarn Hows Wood, then the path quickly swings off right for a sustained pull through the trees. Rising to meet a broader way from the right, keep left for a level spell before resuming up to a boundary wall. The path ascends with it, giving views out across Yewdale to Wetherlam. Levelling out at the top corner, a short path runs left through a gate to idyllically sited Tarn Hows Cottage: the right-hand path runs outside its grounds to a bridle-gate onto its access road. Either way, join its drive just above the house.

Ignore the road rising away and take a gate on the right, sending a fine grassy way across the field. With open views this same track will take you all the way down to Coniston Water. It is at once obvious that woodland on the map here is non-existent. Through a gate above a wood it runs on and down through a gate/stile, earning full-length views of the lake. After a sharp kink left the track resumes, then drops left to a gate and all the way down onto a hedgerowed lane. Go left to Boon Crag National Trust base, joining the B5285 and turning right onto a parallel bridleway. At a junction at the head of Coniston Water simply swing right to remain alongside the road: initially with lake views, you re-enter the village at Yewdale Bridge.

Tarn Hows Cottage

3^{1}2 miles from Coniston

A fascinating exploration of a former copper industry on the flanks of Coniston Old Man

Start Village centre (SD 301975; LA21 8DU), National Park car park
Map OS Explorer 6, English Lakes South West

From the Black Bull cross the adjacent bridge on Church Beck and turn right up a narrow road. Immediately after the Sun Hotel turn right on a short access road between buildings, continuing through a gate and on to bridge a sidestream. A steeper, enclosed climb ascends above Church Beck's wooded ravine. At the top is a gate onto open fellside, and the stony track continues up above the beck past a fine waterfall just before stone-arched Miners Bridge. Cross to a firmer access road and go left up this, passing another waterfall to emerge into Coppermines Valley. Marking the end of the first uphill stage, this fine moment reveals Coniston Old Man rising above a once busy mining scene. Coniston is famous for having been Lakeland's principle copper mining area: at its mid-19th century peak this valley employed over 500 men.

Advance along the unmade road to Coniston Copper Mines at the end. Most prominent building is the white-walled youth hostel in the former mine office: panels explain the industry's story. To the right is restored Bonsor Low Mill, now accommodation. Follow the track left past the hostel, rising above Levers Water Beck to level out with an old slate quarry just to the left. With a waterworks installation in front bear right, ignoring the stony road in favour of a grass path rising right from this junction. Higher up it swings left at a path junction to join a dry mill-race, one of several built to supply waterwheels. Crossing straight over it the path slants up to rejoin the stony road on a hairpin bend, looking down on Paddy End Copper Works backed by the Old Man with its high-level slate quarries. Resume up this, passing an arched mine level and shortly after, looking out for a second mill-race. Marking the walk's high point, double back right on its grassy embankment. With massive views including much of Coniston Water, it ends on a grassy platform beneath the rocky bluff of Kennel Crag.

Revealed in front is the valley of Red Dell Beck, and a grassy path heads off to descend easy slopes ahead. It slants left down to a waterwheel pit at Red Dell Copper Works: the incline above carried water pump rods and winding chains from a higher shaft. Just ahead, a broader path is joined, turning right on it past a vegetation-rich area of fenced shafts. Bridging Red Dell Beck you reach the sizeable remains of Old Engine Shaft, with another wheelpit that operated water pumps and hauled ore tubs from Bonsor Mine. Just past them is the large entrance of Cobbler Hole.

Remain on this old mine track to commence the return, passing above Bonsor East wheelhouse and slanting delightfully across the fellside above your outward route. Ultimately merging into a quarry track in front of spoil heaps, drop right to absorb an access track from old miners' cottages to your right. Rejoining the unmade valley road turn left, briefly retracing outward steps but remain on its firmer course. This drops down off the fell at a cattle-grid, becoming enclosed then surfaced to return to the start.

Coniston Coppermines

4¾ miles from Torver

Hugely colourful country leads to an extended lakeshore ramble

Start *Village centre (SD 283941; LA21 8AZ), village hall car park*
Map *OS Explorer 6, English Lakes South West*

Torver is a small village with two pubs and a deli. From the junction head east on the A5084, quickly taking an enclosed drive right. Before reaching Moor Farm branch left on a similar track, soon reaching a sharp bend right: a bridle-gate on the left sends a more inviting enclosed path away. This runs a delightful course to re-emerge, on through trees in a dip then enclosed again by Torver Beck. It quickly drops down to the former Torver Mill in a beautiful setting at Mill Bridge. Don't follow the drive out but turn right past a barn, the enclosed way swinging left up to a gate onto Torver Low Common. Of two paths rising away, take the left one with the wall. As this swings left the path rises straight ahead, soon revealing Torver Tarn. The path runs its full length, well above the shoreline, with super views back to Dow Crag and Coniston Old Man.

By the modest dam at the far end the path drops slightly to cross the tiny outflow, then take the thinner left branch the short way to meet a broader path. Go left, descending to re-cross the stream and levelling out in the colourful side valley of Mere Beck. A grand stroll leads ultimately to a confluence with Torver Beck. This is crossed by a footbridge, with stepping-stones just downstream by the confluence. On the other side the path rises by a wall to a kissing-gate onto the A5084. Cross to a parking area and turn right on a cart track. This winds up onto Torver Back Common and on to a gate where Coniston Water makes its first real appearance. The main path soon slants down to the wall below, and drops to the shore at Sunny Bank jetty. Turn left on the lakeshore path for a good 1¹4 miles. The shore is never more than a few yards away as you pass through bracken, scrub and scattered woodland, and ultimately a second gate puts you into Torver Common Wood. A fence comes in with a grass enclosure, at the end of which you finally forsake the lakeshore, with Torver jetty just ahead.

Coniston Water is fourth largest of the English lakes, with a string of famous connections. Victorian artist, poet, critic and environmentalist John Ruskin lived at Brantwood, overlooking the lake; Arthur Ransome set his childrens' adventures 'Swallows and Amazons' on and around the lake; while Donald Campbell was the world water speed record breaker who perished attempting to beat his own record here in January 1967. Today the lake is graced by the Victorian steam yacht Gondola and more regular launches.

Turn sharp left on a largely enclosed path between open pasture and woodland. Quickly running to a bridle-gate back into the wood, the path rises gently away, levels out then swings left up to a gate into a sloping pasture. Rising away to a bridle-gate at the top, it runs on to enjoy a walled course to merge into an access track at Brackenbarrow Farm. Follow this left out onto a back road, with the Coniston Fells majestic ahead. From a stile opposite, a faint grassy path curves left down and across a field to a redundant stile with kissing-gate behind, just past which it drops onto the old railway that ran from Foxfield to Coniston. Turn left for a simple stroll back into the village.

Coniston Water

3³4 miles from Water Yeat

A magical amble round unassuming, colourful country off the beaten track

Start *Fairholme Green (SD 286902; LA12 8DW), southernmost of two parking areas on A5084 between Brown Howe car park/WC and hamlet of Water Yeat*
Map *OS Explorer 6, English Lakes South West*

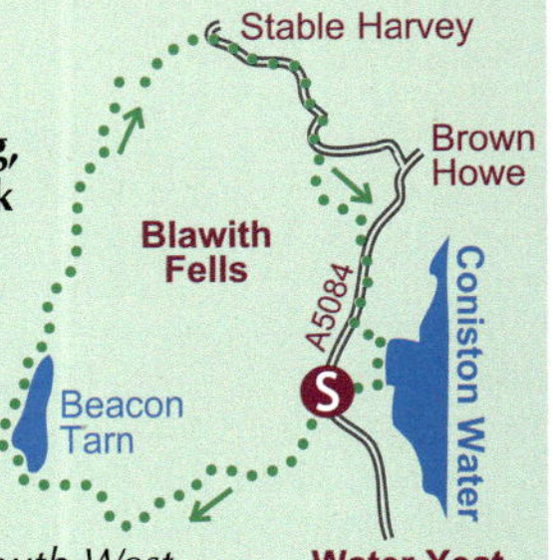

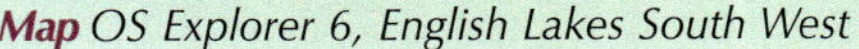

Head south on the road for a few strides to an information panel, where a grassy path bears off right. Quickly crossing a streamlet to merge with another path from the road, it commences a sustained but lovely pull through bracken. Widening views look back over Coniston Water, and up to Coniston Old Man and Wetherlam. The streamlet is crossed a couple of times before easing out, with a few fainter yards alongside rocks at the head of a small marsh. While the path doesn't look to continue, it actually turns sharp left, striding the marsh on stones and rising much clearer again to a knoll. Here is another fork: one runs left while yours bears right onto the brow, easing out to reveal the extensive Blawith Fells ahead, and the top of Slatestone Fell up to your left.

The excellent path now slants left down to a simple bridge on a streamlet. At this junction, cross the bridge and head away on a path with the stream, with a marshy basin to your right. Rising very gently it curves left to fork: the right branch crosses the trickle, but either will suffice as just a minute further comes sudden arrival at the foot of Beacon Tarn. This blue gem is the highlight of the walk, backed by shapely, distant Dow Crag. To resume cross the outflow and follow the tarn's west bank, absorbing a path from Wool Knott and remaining near the bank to the far end. Across the tarn rises 836ft/255m Blawith Beacon.

A slight rise follows to a saddle, with the Coniston Fells dramatically returning. The path drops down to run alongside Red Moss, at the end of which the second half of the descent is made on a super path slanting right through bracken down to the edge of extensive Stable Harvey Moss. On levelling out to a fork, remain on the main path bearing left beneath a small outcrop, curving round the low spur to cross the moss's outflow, Black Beck. Mounting another minor brow, the grassy path quickly meets the sharp bend of an access road. Turn right for a pleasant, traffic-free meander around the common. Leave at a sharp bend left at an information panel: here a grassy path runs straight on, rising marginally. A briefly level section turns sharp left for a slight rise, before a steady drop to run through trees onto the A5084 near a lodge.

Turn right for a few minutes back to the start. To include the lake, a grassy path leaving the first parking area soon runs between reedbeds to the attractive shore. A continuing path runs right, rapidly leaving the lake and running through trees up to a wall gateway back onto the common. Head away, rising gently through bracken to a hollow: while a branch runs straight on, take the main, level one briefly left to a junction, where turn right to cross a tiny brow to reveal the parking area just ahead.

Beacon Tarn

3¹2 miles from Ulpha

**Rugged, unfrequented fell country
- choose a clear day**

Start *Ulpha Bridge
(SD 196930; LA20 6DT),
parking area at edge of
common on south side of bridge*
Map *OS Explorer 6, English Lakes South West*

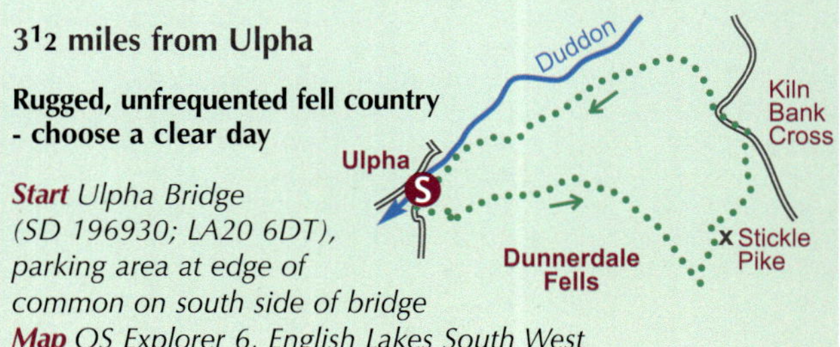

Ulpha is a scattered Duddon Valley community with a Post office/shop and church. Don't cross the cattle-grid to the bridge but head briefly back along the common to an access road going left, rising to a house at Low Birks. Here leave it for a stony path climbing right by a wall to abruptly terminate upon leaving the wall on easier slopes. A grassy continuation bears more faintly right across briefly moister ground, quickly re-establishing itself on better slopes just ahead. It rises left to commence a mercurial course across bracken slopes, with outstanding views over the valley. After a more level section it starts rising gently again to fork alongside a colourful knoll. Stickle Pike has just revealed itself ahead, looking rather intimidating! Turn right here, soon rising more markedly and absorbing a path from the left. At another fork just above, keep left to end abruptly on a knoll, with Stickle Pike still quite daunting.

Your objective is the gentler slope right of the summit cone. Head away across level, mixed ground for less than five minutes, crossing a trickle and along to a second branch of the streamlet. Turn right with this on a faint trod rising to a tiny confluence, where go straight ahead to an obvious little path up steeper ground. This climbs to commence a nice, steady rise with steeper slopes falling right. Reaching the path's high point at some rocks it starts to dip away: instead rise briefly left onto a knoll with stony outcrops. Here double back left on this little spur to gain the foot of the hill's upper cone. With only hints of a path, climb left of the stonier sections onto a platform at a quarried area. Resuming, again keep left of the rougher section to wind steeply up the short way between small outcrops onto another small platform by jagged rocks. Above this you quickly emerge onto easier ground, with the sturdy summit cairn at 1230ft/375m just a minute further up to the left.

Arrival on this characterful summit is an exhilarating moment. Outstanding views range from the Scafells in the heart of Lakeland down to the Duddon Estuary and Morecambe Bay, while Stickle Tarn is contrastingly close down to the right. Leave on a well-worn path dropping right in the tarn's direction. Initially stony, it slants onto easier ground to run left the short way to a dip, with the reedy little tarn just to your right. The onward path resumes the descent, forking but merging to approach a parking area on the summit of Kiln Bank Cross road. Whilst the onward route is left on the road, avoid tarmac for longer by crossing an incoming path and continuing on a path down bracken flanks to join the road lower down.

Go left down to a wall and cattle-grid, beneath which a path is signed left across open pasture. Keeping left of a minor bouldery scarp, a thin path forms to drop to a corner stile onto a cart track. This runs left for a grand, gentle descent towards the valley, eventually dropping right onto another track, and left through a gate into Birks Wood. Almost at once drop right on a broad path to a gate at the bottom by the river. Now simply trace the Duddon downstream through grassy pasture to a wall-stile alongside the bridge.

Looking up the Duddon Valley

3^{1}2 miles from Seathwaite

A beautiful wooded ravine within the secretive Duddon Valley

Start Village centre (SD 228960; LA20 6ED), parish room car park by church
Map *OS Explorer 6, English Lakes South West*

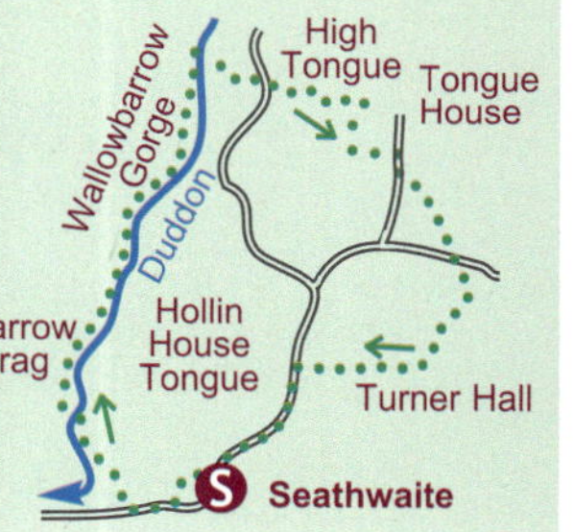

Tiny Seathwaite is the heart of the Duddon Valley. From the parish room go a few strides right to Holy Trinity church, opposite which a path squeezes into trees above Tarn Beck. A few yards left is a stile into a field, turning downstream the short way to a path junction. Go left across the field to a gate, and on through gates onto the road opposite the Newfield Inn. Turn right a short way to the old schoolhouse, and a gate set back on the right sends a path to a footbridge on Tarn Beck. Two paths head away left: the lower traces the beck to a confluence with the Duddon, then upstream with it; the upper one through Tongue Wood rejoins by the river. A little further you reach a gate to cross an arched bridge on the river.

Turn right to begin a memorable trek through Wallowbarrow Gorge, soon crossing a wall-stile. The first section sees the path negotiate boulders beneath steep, rugged slopes, while the Duddon runs a magical course highlighted at a waterfall into a deep pool. Slow progress leads to easier going as the path climbs away from the river and over a stile. Joined by a deer fence this continues at a higher level. As trees thin out you gain a colourful knoll, with views over the deep wooded gorge to Dow Crag and Walna Scar. The path runs on, finally leaving the deer fence as you drop right to a footbridge on Grassguards Gill. Over a stile, a minute further you arrive at Fickle Steps. These sturdy boulders carry you across the river with the help of a wire handrail (other than in spate).

Across, take the left-hand path rising away, easing to slant right up bracken slopes onto the valley road. In springtime either side of this tarmac strip boasts an unrivalled bluebell display. Cross to the left-hand grassy path heading away beneath a crag under High Tongue. Just ahead it forks right to pass a modest rocky knoll and on through scattered trees back into the open. It drops to a gateway in an old wall and then on beneath a wooded, craggy bank, past a barn to a cottage at Thrang. From a small gate on its near side, leave by a gate a few yards to the right. A faint grassy way crosses the field, dropping left to a footbridge on Tarn Beck.

Joining an access road, go right until a gate on the left just after a sidestream. Follow the stream on your left through a couple of pathless fields, then from a gate rise away with a wall on your right, it transferring to your left side to rise to a gate by a barn onto an access road. Of the two options to your left, take the right-hand one just a few yards to a gate on the right, and another grassy way crosses a field to a gate above High Moss. Bear right of the house to join and follow its drive across two fields to approach Turner Hall Farm. In the yard in front go right on the access road, around the farm and down to a surfaced access road. Go right to join the valley road, then left for a few minutes close by Tarn Beck to finish.

The path at High Tongue

3 miles from Hardknott Pass

A dramatically sited Roman fort in the mountainous basin of the River Esk

Start *Jubilee Bridge (NY 213011; CA19 1TH), car park above cattle-grid at foot of pass*
Map *OS Explorer 6, English Lakes South West*

Cross the cattle-grid and down over Hardknott Gill to an old phonebox, where turn right on Brotherilkeld's drive. En route you re-cross the beck to join the River Esk. Don't enter the farmyard but bear left to the river, and through a kissing-gate a path runs grandly between the youthful Esk and sheep pastures. Bowfell's pyramid draws the eye ahead, with the Scafell group over to the left and Hard Knott's rugged flank on your right. Further, you meet a kissing-gate alongside a gate as the river swings off. The onward grassy track crosses open pasture to a gate in the wall ahead, then continues, latterly rising slightly to another gate/stile.

This is your turning point, so don't pass through but double back sharply right. Initially pathless, simply maintain a level course over mixed ground to find a path forming as you approach bracken. From hereon the way is clear, running on between a massive boulder and a small pool to a wall junction. Through the gate the path hugs the wallside, dropping a little then on through another gate and on towards the rear of the farm. Don't drop down but continue above the wall, soon rising briefly to a gate/stile on a brow. Though the start is just a minute beyond the stile, ignore it in favour of a grassy wallside path rising left through bracken. This soon diverges from the wall and up to a stile in the wall above. Heading away, within yards a cross-paths is met: turn left on the broad, more steeply climbing branch. The going soon eases and you arrive outside the western gateway of the Roman fort of Hardknott Castle.

The Romans' Mediobogdum is a magnificent site astride their route from Glannoventa at Ravenglass to Galava at Ambleside. Its strategic position on Hardknott Pass overlooks all of Eskdale down to the coast. Modern day travellers are still challenged by hairpin bends and an infamous 33% gradient section of this narrow, snaking road over the fells. The Principia (headquarters) sits at the centre of the fort, while broad gateways occupy all four sides. From the northern one a walk of just 50 yards puts you on an airy perch where a lone holly boasts the finest view in Lakeland, with the peaks of Upper Eskdale arrayed above your earlier route far below.

Leave by the southern gateway, the path swinging left to the remains of the bath-house. Around its side forsake the onward path to a parking area, and drop immediately right onto the road. Turn right, and a minute after an information panel in a parking area, the road bends sharp left: here take the grassy path ahead, within a minute taking you back to the earlier cross-paths. This time take the left branch down onto the road at a wall corner. Most of the remaining descent can be enjoyed on grass paths through bracken that short-cut the road's bends, soon returning you to the start.

Hard Knott from the Roman fort

3¹₂ miles from Boot

Excellent, easy paths trace a beautiful river

Start *Dalegarth Station (NY 173007; CA19 1TF) car park just west of village*
Map *OS Explorer 6, English Lakes South West*

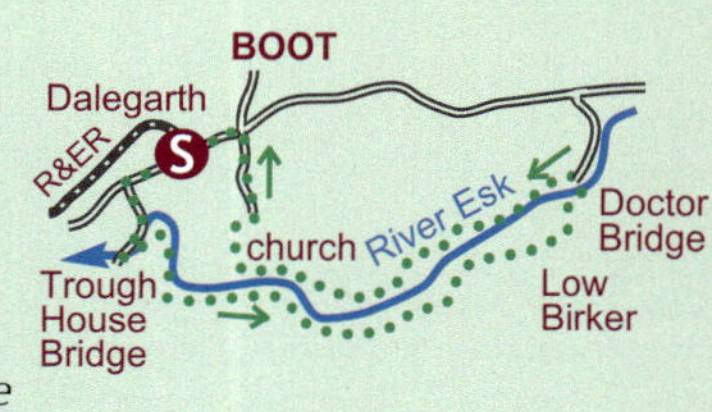

For a note on the Ravenglass & Eskdale Railway see page 58. Rejoin the road and turn right for a couple of minutes to a junction at a former school of 1863. Go left past the war memorial down to the wooded environs of Trough House Bridge on the River Esk. The Esk rises as a mountain stream amid England's highest fells, and descends some 2000 feet in just 5 miles: your acquaintance with it enjoys a more sedate passage between wooded banks and green pastures. Across, a bridle-gate on the left sends a firm path upstream, soon deflected right with inflowing Stanley Gill. A gate puts you into its wooded environs, where cross by footbridge or stepping-stones and out through a gate beyond. The left-hand path upstream quickly arrives opposite St Catherine's church. Through a gate in the fence ignore the stepping-stones and resume upstream to the environs of Gill Force, where the Esk forms crystal-clear pools between rocky walls. Just beyond is a footbridge whose girders supported a mineral tramway that extended from Dalegarth to serve iron ore mines in a short-lived venture around 1880.

The path swings right to a junction above, where a branch runs left to the bridge. Ignore this and go right, rising to another junction: ignore the gate on the right and go left on a path through trees. Broadening into a track it runs on with craggy slopes above and views to Bowfell and Scafell. At a plantation fronting a reedy pool, a continuing green path slants gently left down and on to a gate and footbridge on another inflowing stream, Force Gill. Resuming, your route becomes a walled way with glorious views over the valley. As the house at Low Birker appears ahead, a bridle-gate on the left sends a path slanting left beneath it to join its driveway at the other side. Go left on this the short way to rejoin the river just before stone-arched Doctor Bridge.

Cross and leave the access road by a gate sending a super path downstream with the Esk. Emerging into open pasture, it continues beneath a colourful bank for a considerable time, never far from the river. Note also the splendid waterfall of Birker Force between crags on the skyline across the river. Ignoring branches right it runs a foolproof course through this colourful country, at times briefly enclosed by walls and encountering occasional small gates. Later, with a grassy pasture ahead, the path bears right to by-pass a bend of the river, quickly rejoining it just above Gill Force. Drop down to the girder bridge to enjoy the surroundings, then resume downstream on the old tramway's course to a pair of gates.

While the tramway runs right, use the left-hand gate for a last riverside section to the church in its idyllic setting. Note the carved gravestone of Tommy Dobson, a celebrated master of the Ennerdale Foxhounds. Finally forsaking the Esk, follow the access road right, becoming surfaced at the hamlet of Church House and out to a crossroads at Brook House Inn on the edge of Boot. The start is just two minutes to the left.

Boot church

3³⁄4 miles from Boot

Absorbing peat cutters' paths access a remote tarn on a colourful fellside with stupendous Eskdale views

Start Dalegarth Station
(NY 173007; CA19 1TF)
car park just west of village
Map OS Explorer 6,
English Lakes South West

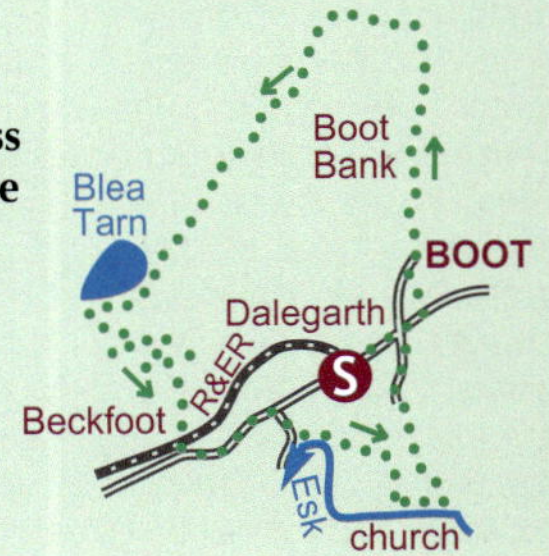

Dalegarth is terminus of the Ravenglass & Eskdale Railway, opened in 1875 to transport iron ore from mines on the fells above Boot to the main line on the coast. Acquired by a preservation society in 1960, today it carries thousands of visitors along its colourful, narrow-gauge course affectionately known as La'al (Little) Ratty. Rejoin the road and turn left the short way to a crossroads at Brook House Inn. A minute further turn left up an inviting green way between walls to the road at the entrance to Boot. This hamlet features the Boot Inn and a seasonal gift shop. Continue the short way to the end, crossing a packhorse bridge on Whillan Beck to Eskdale Cornmill. Abandoned in the 1930s, it was left largely undisturbed and restored for visitors in 1985. Its two waterwheels were joined by a third in 2017 to provide hydroelectricity.

Just in front, a gate sends a path onto the open fell. Go right, rising through bracken between widely spaced walls. It continues slanting up Boot Bank, with excellent views over the village and valley to the cone of Harter Fell and the high peaks of the Scafells and Bowfell. Eventually escaping walls the way slants up into a scattering of stone huts where freshly cut peat was once stored. Before the last one, leave the bridleway for a grassier left branch on softer ground. Within 100 yards a sunken way merges from the final hut to your right, and here you twice cross a streamlet before heading off across the moor to a cairn.

The path continues to a larger cairn, then runs on as a super green way to rise slightly past a fenced, deep shaft from 19th century iron ore mining. Passing through a low wall you arrive at a large marshy hollow, and the path runs along its right side. At a stone hut ignore a branch rising right, and towards the end your path rises to a massive cairn at a path crossroads in a small nick. The main path drops left down a neat groove, revealing the large, unfrequented Blea Tarn as it drops down to traverse its shore. From a few boulders at the end a path bears left past a tiny marsh to transform into a grassy way through bracken. Eskdale returns in style as the descent commences, quickly passing an old peat hut. From a junction just beneath it keep right on the main path, with the village re-appearing. The path engages a series of mercurial grassy zigzags to rapidly return to the valley. At the bottom it drops right to a gate onto the railway at Beckfoot, crossing to join the parallel road.

Go left over Whillan Beck to a junction at a former school of 1863. Though the start is just two minutes further, turn right past the war memorial to quickly leave by a gate on the left. An enclosed bridleway runs a fine course along the valley floor to an access road, where turn right to the idyllic riverside setting of St Margaret's church. A path runs upstream with the Esk a short way to a gate, where turn left through another onto a walled way. This former mineral tramway course runs along to rejoin the access road at the hamlet at Church House. Go right out to Brook House Inn, and left the couple of minutes back to the station.

La'al Ratty

4½ miles from Nether Wasdale

Low-level walking with stunning views

Start *Cinderdale Bridge
(NY 128038; CA20 1ET),
car park off junction
just east of village centre*
Map *OS Explorer 6, English Lakes South West*

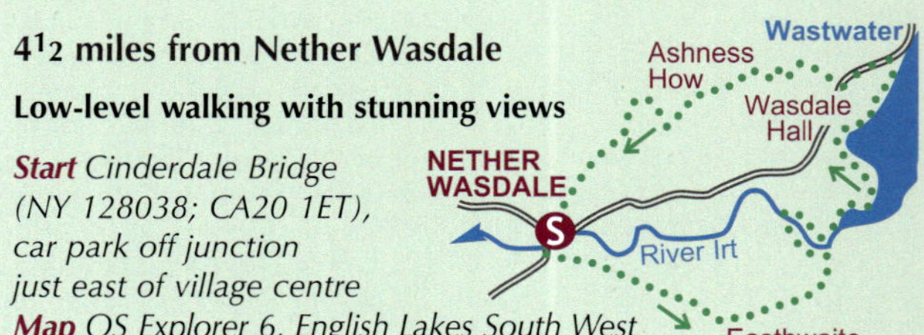

The tiny village of Nether Wasdale features a brace of pubs, the Strands and the Screes, facing each other across green spaces. From the junction take the Santon Bridge road over Forest Bridge on the River Irt. Almost at once turn left on a lengthy, unsurfaced access road all the way to Easthwaite Farm, with Whin Rigg towering behind. En route the Wasdale fells of Buckbarrow, Middle Fell, Yewbarrow, Kirk Fell and Great Gable are arrayed beyond unseen Wastwater. Through the farm gate don't advance into the yard, but turn right up a tiny, walled green way to a kissing-gate. The path then slants left up into the yard at the rear, where cross to a gate onto the foot of the open fell, and turn left.

A grassy path rises slightly from the intake wall, and runs on through bracken before contouring across to join the wall. The lake appears ahead and your path crosses the little ravine of Greathall Gill, with its small waterfall. Immediately behind it the wall's high point is also the high point of the walk, now with glorious views of the mountain-backed lake and the outflowing River Irt. Remain just above the wall as the path crosses to rejoin it, then descending to an access track by the river. Go left through a kissing-gate and leave by another into trees on the right. This runs with the river, out of the trees, and along the bank to stone-arched Lund Bridge.

Across, leave by a kissing-gate on the right, and a firm path heads away through Low Wood. The river is rejoined to trace it upstream to the lakefoot, reached on passing a romantically sited boathouse. The path runs grandly on the shore, enjoying stunning views over England's deepest lake: while the prospect up its length to the dalehead peaks earned the acclaim of England's finest view, the celebrated Wastwater Screes tumbling into its waters to your right are equally impressive. Emerging from the wood into the parkland of Wasdale Hall, the path advances on the shore beneath the splendid house of 1829, long used as a youth hostel. The path remains by the shore into trees, then a field and finally through rhododendrons to a small gate from where it rises the few yards left onto a road. There is a brief glimpse of Scafell Pike at this point.

Bid farewell to Wastwater and double back left on the road, over a cattle-grid out of open country. After a few short minutes, take a walled cart track rising right into woodland. This runs on to a gate/stile into the open country of Ashness How. A green track bears away left, moist in parts as it runs along to meet a firmer track. Go left on this, improving as it meanders along to a corner gate/stile. An enclosed grass track heads away to a junction of such ways, where turn right. This runs grandly on through a gate to another such junction. Turn left here, quickly running along to cross Scale Bridge on Cinderdale Beck. Cross the field centre behind to a gate, and go left on a grassy wallside way. This runs all the way to Mill Place, whose drive leads out the short way to the junction at the start.

3 miles from Wasdale Head

Stunning Wasdale views from an easy mountainside path

Start Hamlet centre (NY 186087; CA20 1EX), car park on green 100 yards short of hotel
Map OS Explorer 6, English Lakes South West

Wasdale Head is the most dramatically sited settlement in Lakeland, occupying the flat valley head between Wastwater and a horseshoe of rugged peaks. Focal point is the Wasdale Head Inn, an iconic hostelry at the birthplace of English mountaineering. The surrounding mountains include some of England's finest, notably Great Gable, Pillar, Scafell and the highest of them all, Scafell Pike. From the hotel advance along the continuing access road, but turn immediately right through a bridle-gate. An enclosed path runs the short way to St Olaf's tiny church shrouded in yew trees beneath Lingmell's dark flank. An etched window depicts the famous climbers' landmark of Napes Needle on Great Gable, while outside are gravestones of climbers killed on the surrounding peaks.

Emerging at the other side, turn right on the walled access track the short way to the parking area on the green, emerging by the old vicarage. Continue along the road out for just 100 yards, and as it bends sharp right after the tiny former school, take the left-hand of adjacent bridle-gates. A grassy path heads away across the flat pasture, between gorse bushes and along to a footbridge on Lingmell Beck. Given the girth of its stony bed, surprisingly this principal feeder of Wastwater is normally dry other than after heavy rain, having sunk below ground a little further upstream.

Across, a kissing-gate on the right sends the main path slanting steadily up the fellside. Yewbarrow rises steeply across the valley, while Wastwater rapidly appears ahead. The path rises to a kissing-gate in a descending wall, then resumes its slant for some time, with expanding dramatic views. The path eases out as it gains a broad spur descending from Lingmell. At this high point of the walk the path levels out to reveal a magnificent view into Lingmell Gill leading the eye up to the newly revealed Scafell Pike, fronted by the rocky wall of Pikes Crag: to its right is its sidekick Scafell. The path runs grandly on the short way into the enclave of the gill, meeting another path just beneath a kissing-gate in a wall.

Double back right here to commence a quick return to the valley on the well-built path in company with the beck. Lower down, a kissing-gate in a fence transfers you into a grassy pasture: ignore a left branch to a footbridge on the beck and continue down to another kissing-gate. The path now drops enclosed above the beck to emerge by a bridge carrying Wasdale Head Hall Farm access road. Go straight ahead over a cattle-grid and on past the Lake Head car park/WC, soon being joined by the campsite & shop access road to bridge Mosedale Beck onto the valley road. Turn right for a few minutes as far as Down in the Dale Bridge on Mosedale Beck. Don't cross but take a kissing-gate on the left sending a grassy path upstream close by the beck. This runs along via an intervening gate to arrive opposite the hotel. Just ahead, the tapering enclosure draws you to an arched packhorse bridge on the beck, across which turn right back into the hamlet.

Wasdale Head Inn

3$\frac{1}{4}$ miles from Dungeon Ghyll

**Easy walking to a charming tarn
in peerless mountain surroundings**

Start *Dungeon Ghyll Old Hotel, terminus
of B5343, Great Langdale (NY 285060;
LA22 9JY), National Trust car park*
Map *OS Explorer 6, English Lakes South West*

Return to the road and turn right then sharp left. At the first bend a gate on the left leads into a campsite, and follow the drive away. At the end of the parking area turn off to a small footbridge into trees on the right, from where a path rises out of the site via kissing-gates, up a wooded bank. Continue up a field, through a kissing-gate into a wood and out via a final gate onto the grassy fellside. A stony, zizgagging climb ensues with a wall to your right. Stunning views look back to the Langdale Pikes, with Crinkle Crags and Bowfell at the dalehead. Towards the top the Blea Tarn road comes in alongside, and the slope eases to gain the summit of the 735ft/224m pass linking Great Langdale and Little Langdale: Blea Tarn makes its appearance in its delectable bowl ahead. Take a kissing-gate on the right to gain the crest at a cattle-grid.

Cross the road, not the grid, and descend briefly to a bridle-gate in the wall. A broad path heads away above a fence, bound for the tarn: up to the left is craggy Side Pike on Lingmoor Fell. The path runs to a bridle-gate into the tarn's wooded surrounds, and a little branch left leads to a charming promontory. Resuming, fork left at the end of the tarn, over a footbridge on the outflow and along to a wall-gate, with the tarn now a perfect foreground to the Langdale Pikes. The path rises to the road at a gate opposite a car park. Turn left on its meandering course back to the pass, passing Bleatarn House, only habitation in this upland valley. At the road top cross the cattle-grid to retrace opening steps, relishing the prospect of the Pikes dominating the extraordinary Langdale scene.